How to Draw HORSES & PONIES

Learn to draw 20 horse and pony breeds, step by easy step, shape by simple shape!

Illustrated by Russell Farrell

Walter Foster Jr.

Getting Started

When you look closely at the drawings in this book, you'll notice that they're made up of basic shapes, such as circles, ovals, and triangles. To draw any horse and pony, just start with simple shapes as you see here. It's easy and fun!

Circles are one way to start a horse's head, chest, and hips.

Ovals make good profile heads and muzzles.

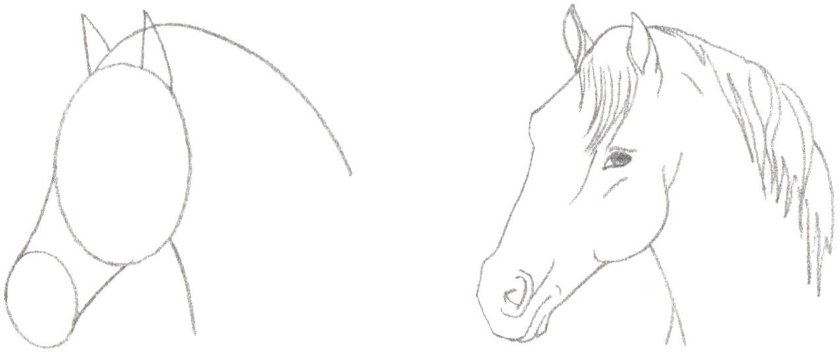

Triangles are perfect for upright ears!

Tips

There's more than one way to bring your four-legged friends to life on paper—you can use crayons, markers, or pencils. Just be sure you have black, brown, and white, plus yellow, orange, red, and blue.

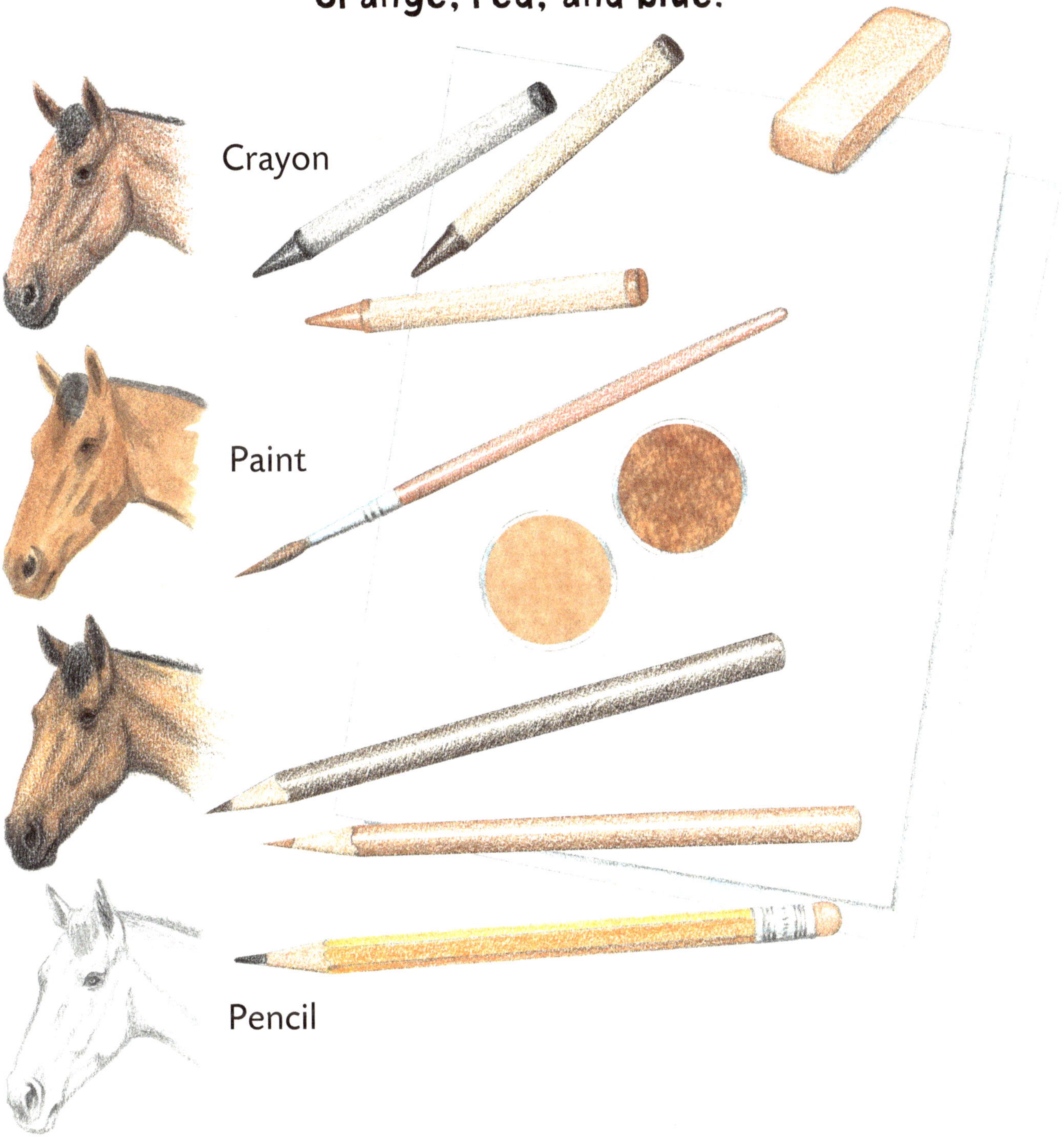

Hanoverian Foal

Start this long-legged baby with two circles for the body. Then finish with a short, brushlike tail and a stiff, upright mane.

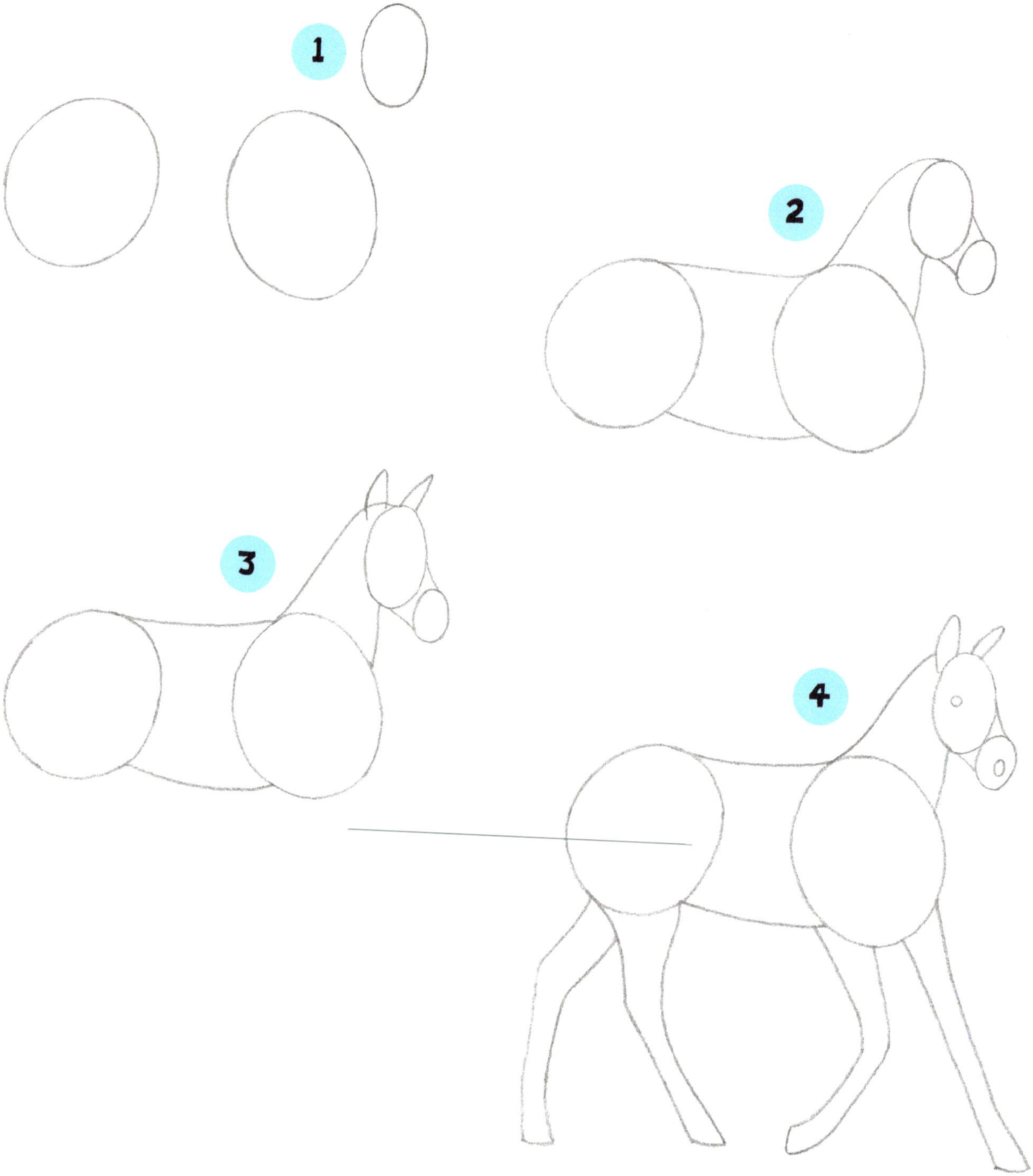

5

6

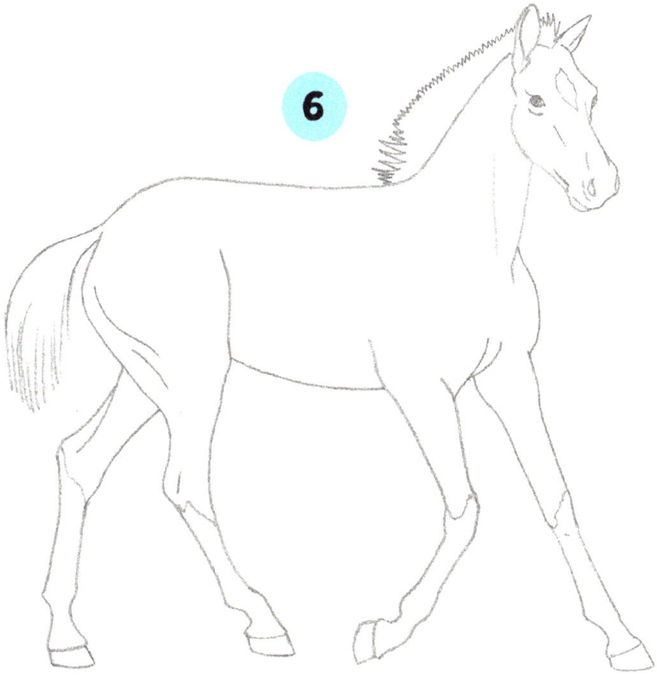

7

fun fact

The first Hanoverians worked as carriage and military horses. But the Hanoverian is now one of the most important sport horse breeds. With their long stride, powerful action, and excellent jumping skills, they have won many world championships, including a number of Olympic medals and more World Cups than any other breed!

Pinto

This breed has a cool patterned coat that sets it apart! A Quarter Horse or Thoroughbred Pinto can also be called a "Paint."

1

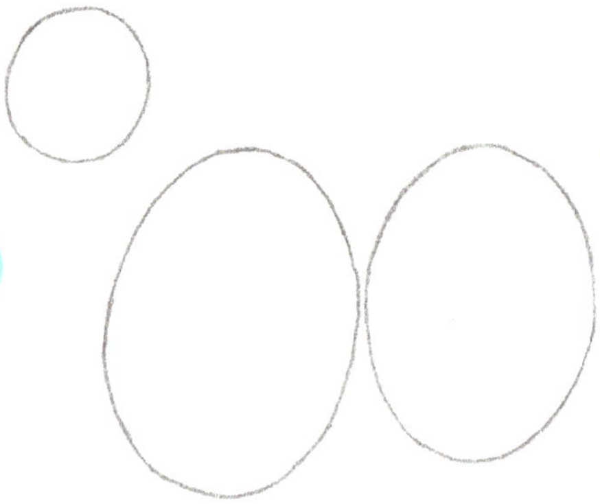

2

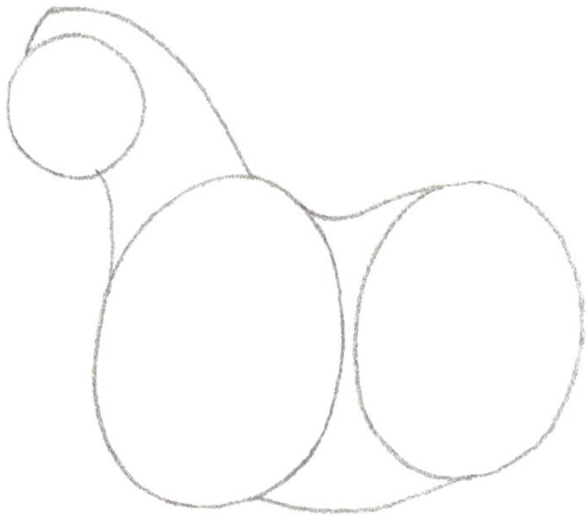

3

4

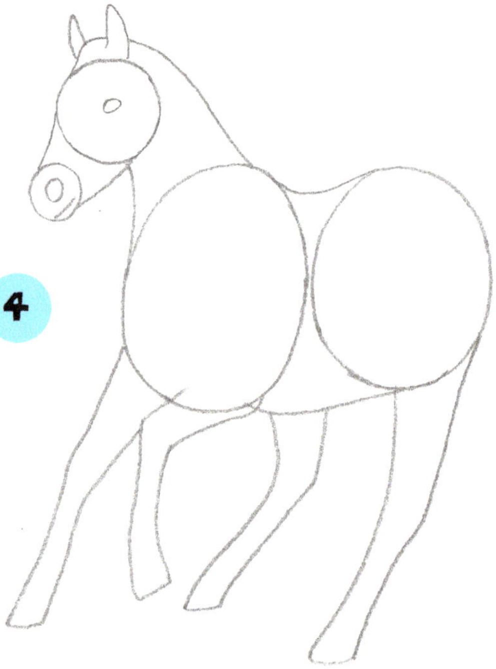

fun fact

Pintos get their name from the Spanish word *pintado,* which means "painted."

5

6

7

Welsh Mountain Pony

This little foal is as cute as can be! First draw its sturdy, round body. Then add super long legs!

1

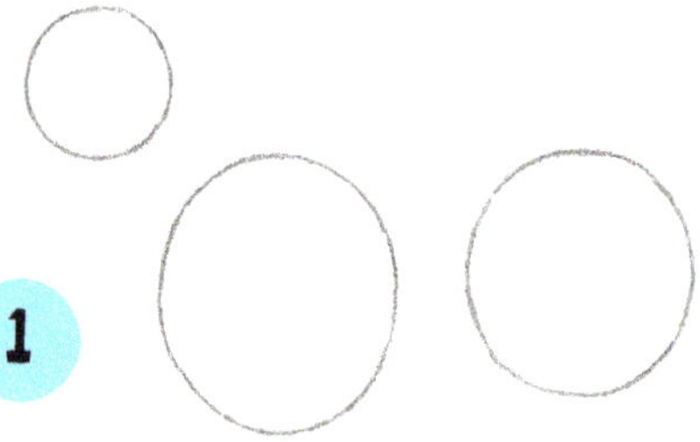

2

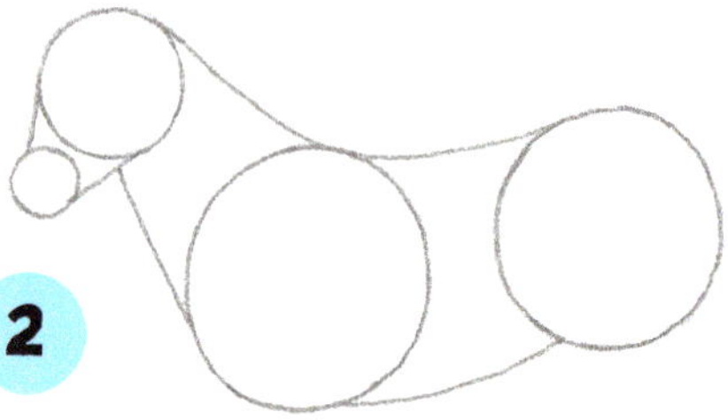

3

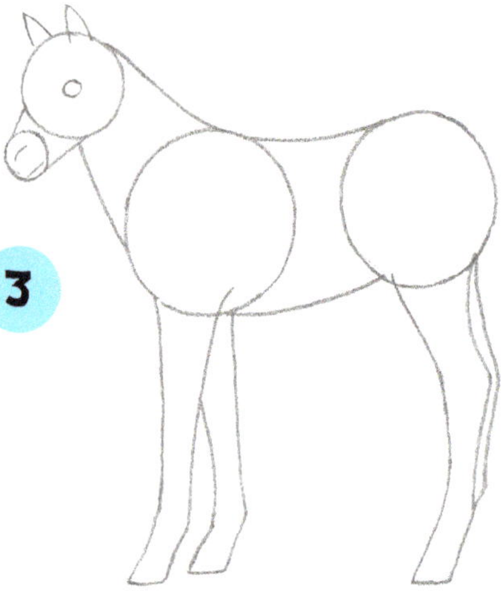

4

5

6

Norwegian Fjord Pony

This primitive-looking pony has zebra stripes on its legs and a dark stripe on its back that goes right through its mane!

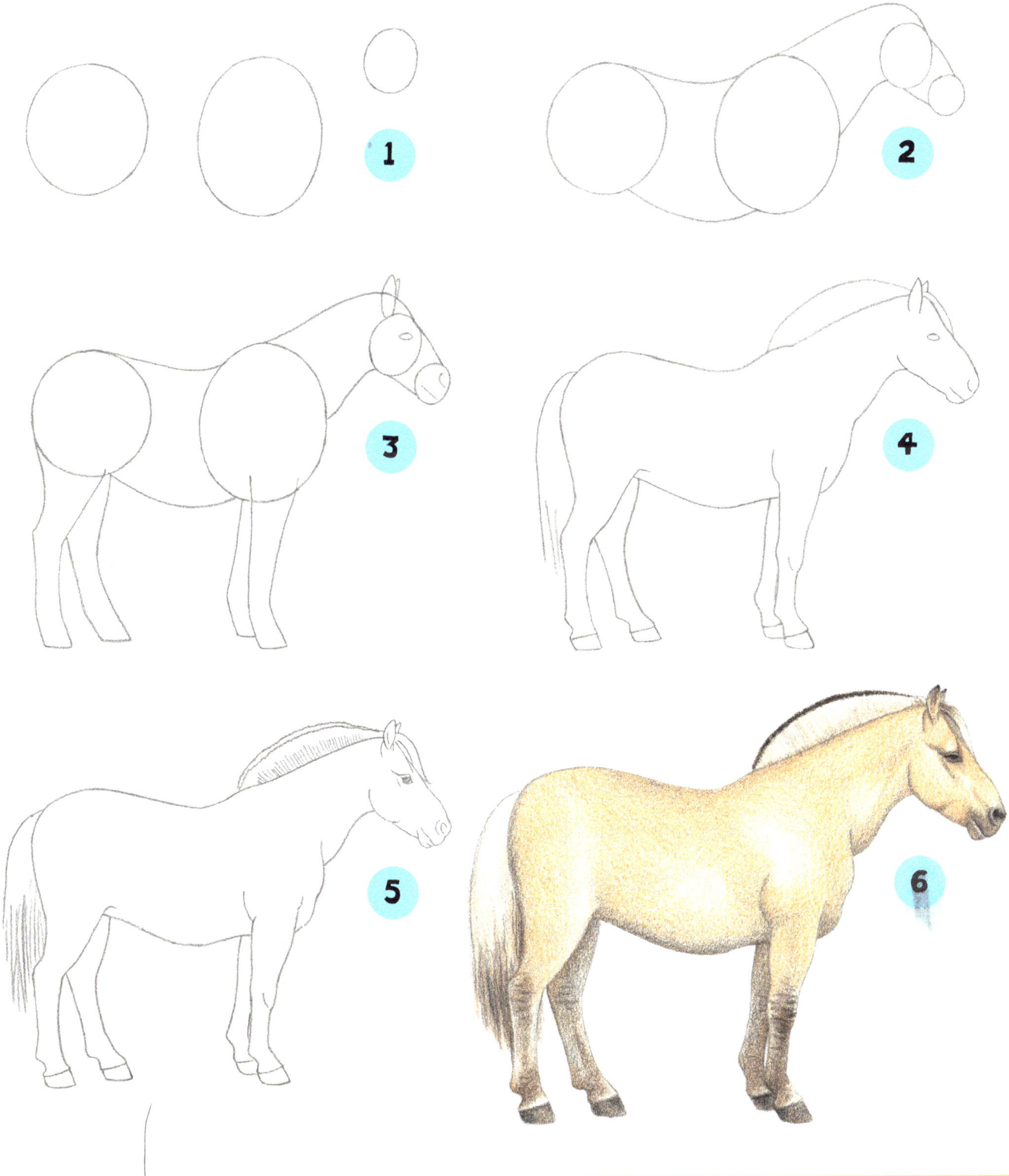

Clydesdale

The clydesdale is a big and powerful draft horse, with long leg hairs—called "feathers"—that almost cover its hooves!

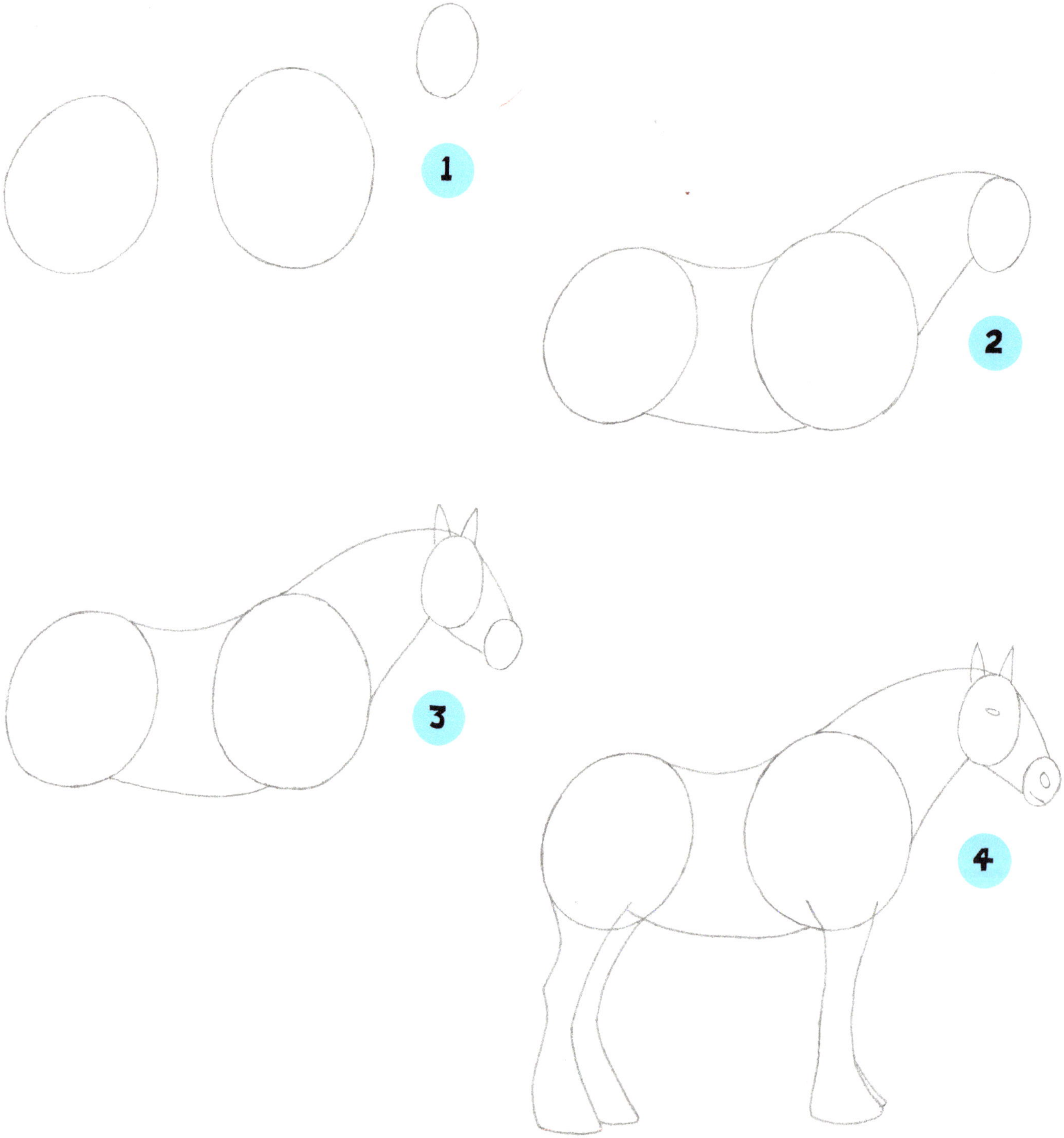

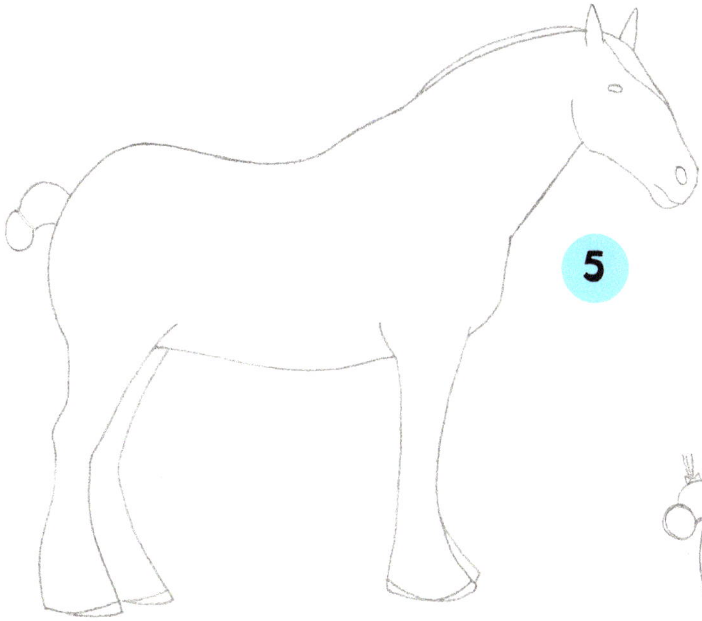

5

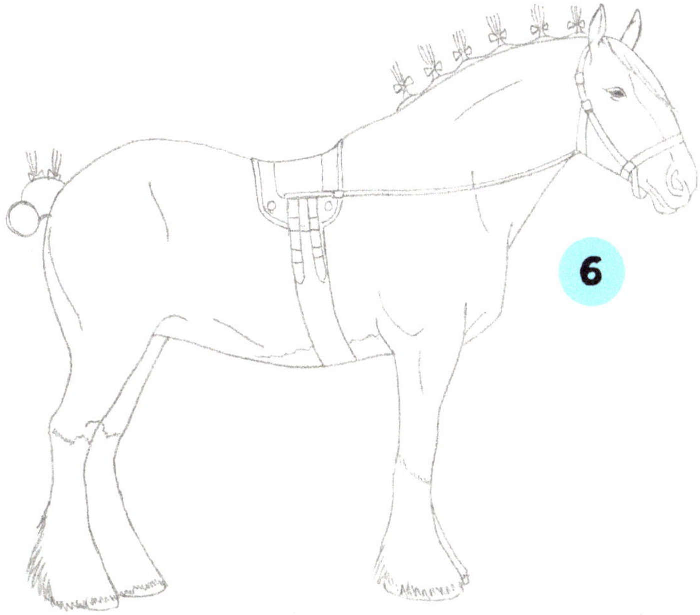

6

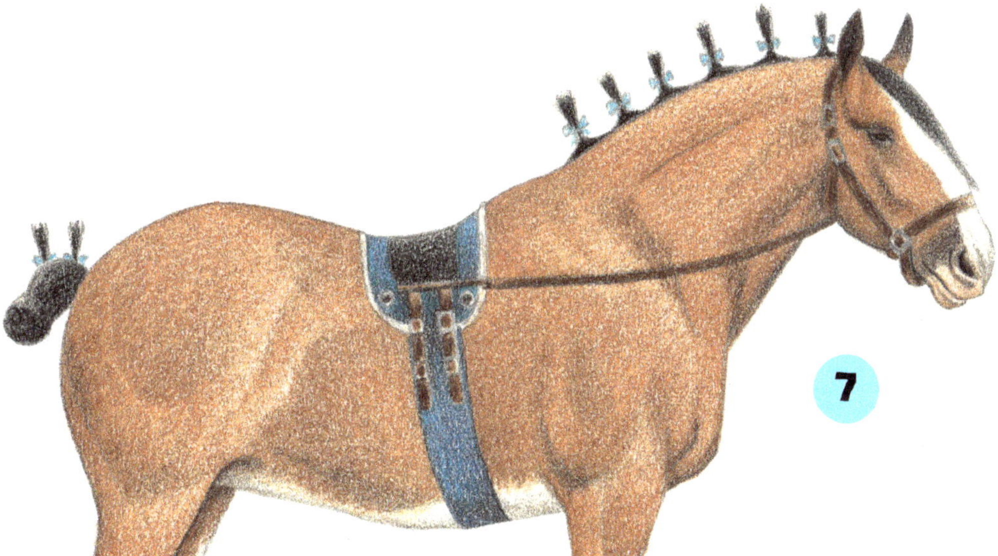

7

Arabian

Its delicate, dished profile, large eyes and nostrils, and small, pointed ears give the Arabian a noble and gentle appearance.

1

2

3

4

fun fact

The Arabian is the world's oldest and purest breed. Bedouin tribes in Arabia first bred these horses 4,000 years ago, using them for transportation. To protect their horses from extreme desert temperatures (and thieves), the Bedouins kept the Arabians in their tents, sleeping, resting, and eating with their steeds by their side.

5

Noriker

An ancient Austrian draft breed (heavy workhorse), the Noriker is strong and stocky, with a long silky mane, tail, and forelock.

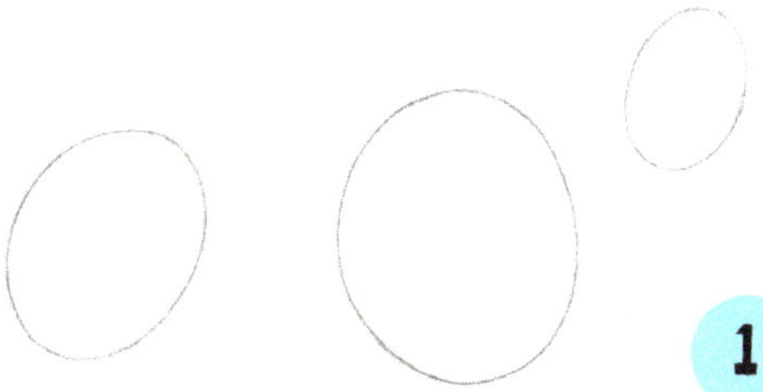

1

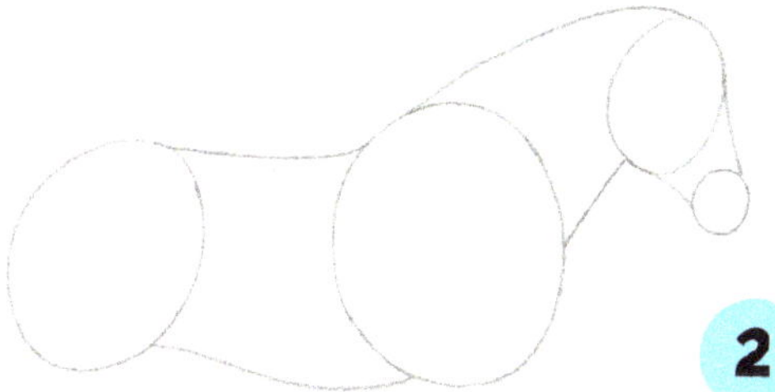

2

3

4

5

6

American Saddlebred

This high-spirited horse shows off its proud style with a high-flying tail and a prancing step!

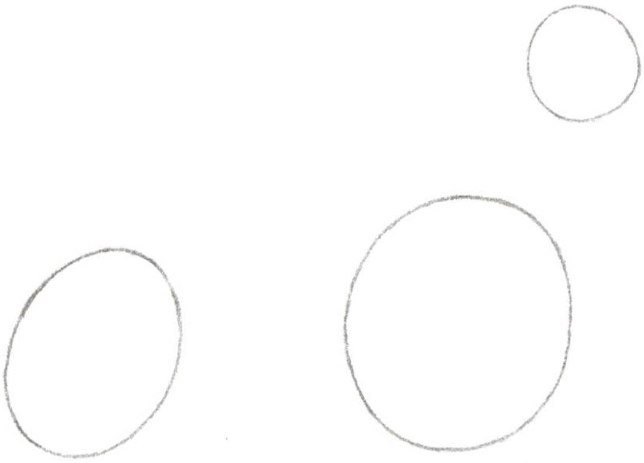

1

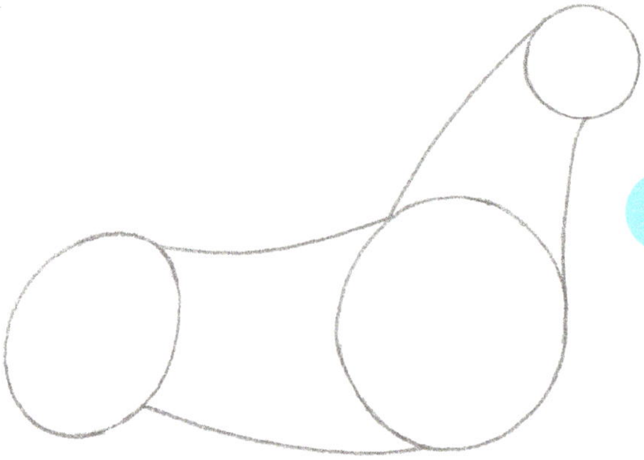

2

3

4

fun fact

The Saddlebred not only walks, trots, and canters—it can also perform two additional smooth, easy-riding gaits: *slow gait* and *rack*. Some horses can carry out the five gaits naturally at birth, but others must be trained to perform the two special gaits.

5

6

7

Morgan

Small but super strong and hardy, the Morgan has a draft horse's muscular hindquarters but thinner legs and an elegant face.

1

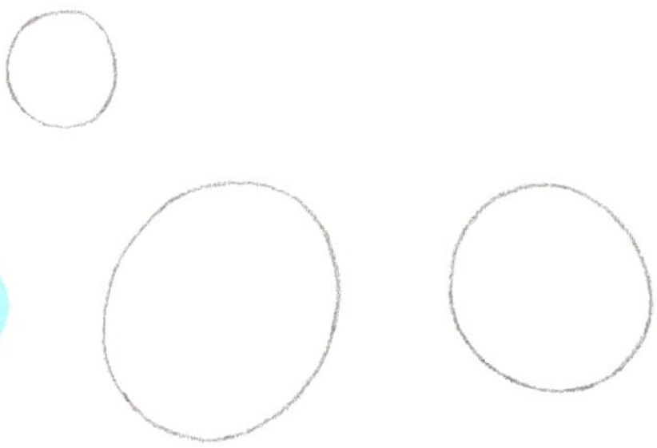

2

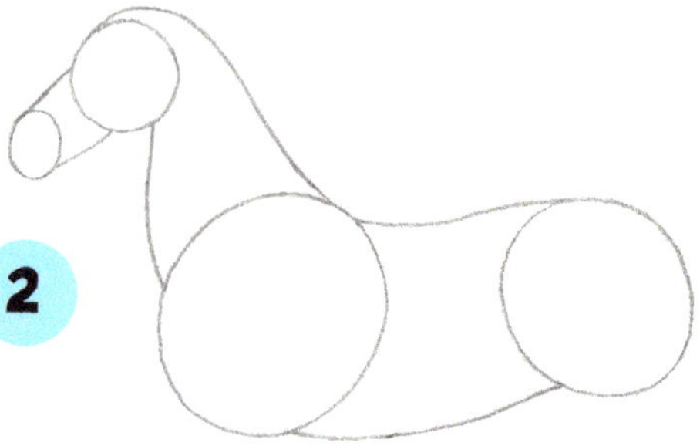

3

4

5

6

Thoroughbred

The fastest breed in the world, the athletic and courageous Thoroughbred can run and jump for miles and miles!

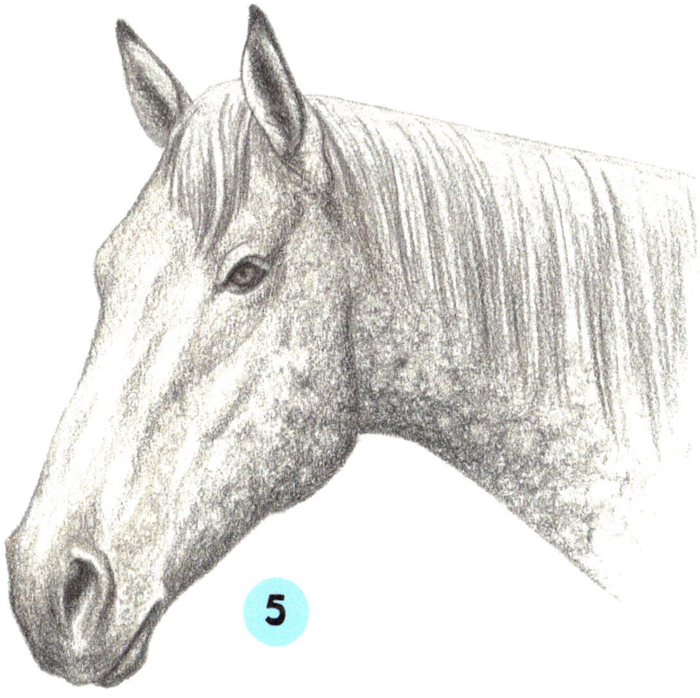

fun fact

Every Thoroughbred racehorse celebrates its birthday on New Year's day. A newborn is considered a foal until January 1st of the year after it is born; then it's called a "yearling."

Friesian

Rapunzel would envy the long, flowing locks of this solid black Friesian—a heavy draft horse from the Netherlands.

1

2

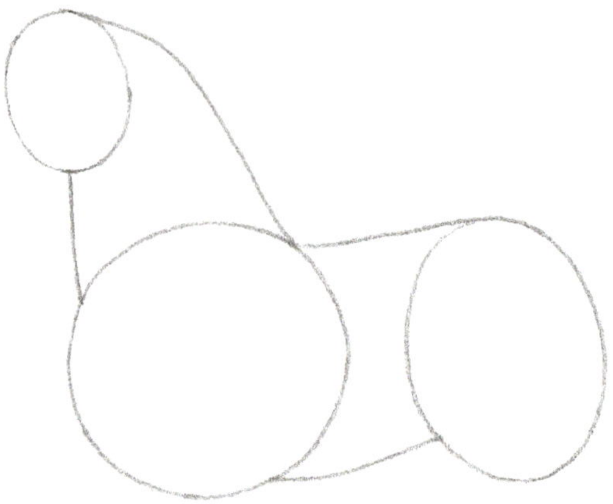

3

4

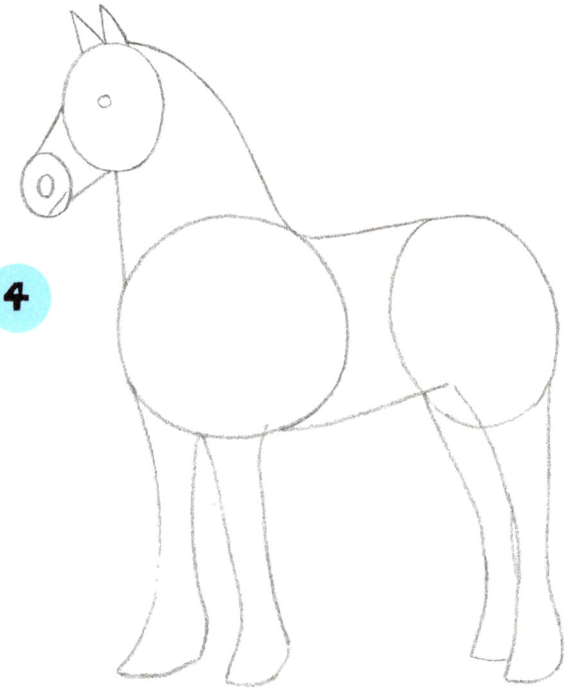

fun fact

This breed has been around for a long time. Documents describing its magnificent characteristics date back to 1200!

5

6

7

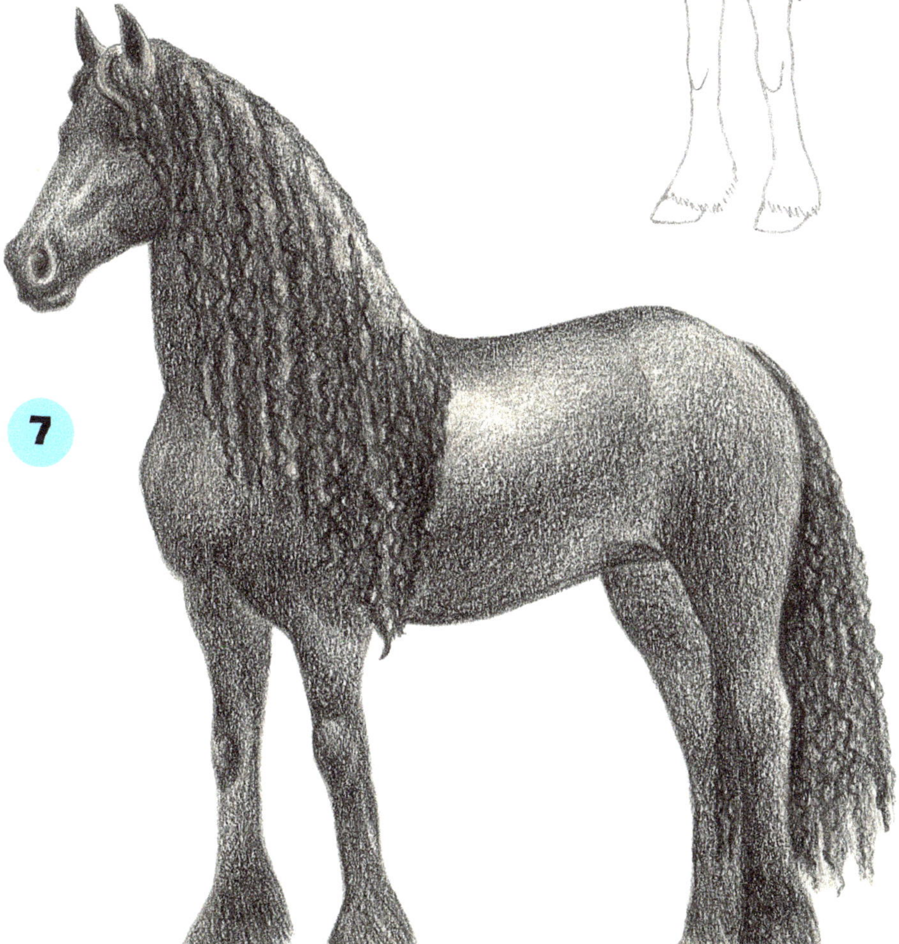

Shetland Pony

A popular breed for pony-loving kids, the adorable Shetland is tiny but tough, with a round belly and short, stocky legs.

Kathiawari

This narrowly built horse from India has distinctive ears that curve inward until their tips actually touch!

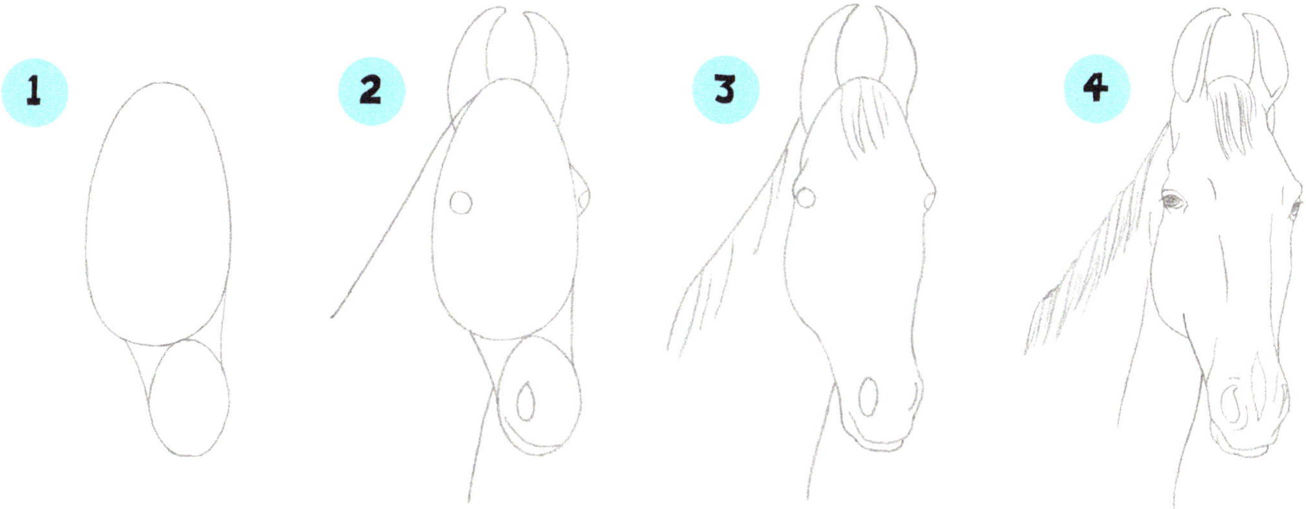

fun fact

This horse is small, but it's also tough, which is why the Kathiawari is popular with tent-pegging athletes. Originally a way to practice wild boar hunting, tent pegging is now a popular sport in India. To play the game, an athlete rides to the middle of an arena and, while on horseback, uses the tip of a lance to pick up a small wooden block—or peg. Picking up the peg earns the rider half a point; picking up the peg and carrying it to the opposite corner of the arena earns a full point.

Appaloosa

The easy-going Appaloosa is awash in spots! Along with its frosted coat pattern, it has a multi-shaded tail.

1

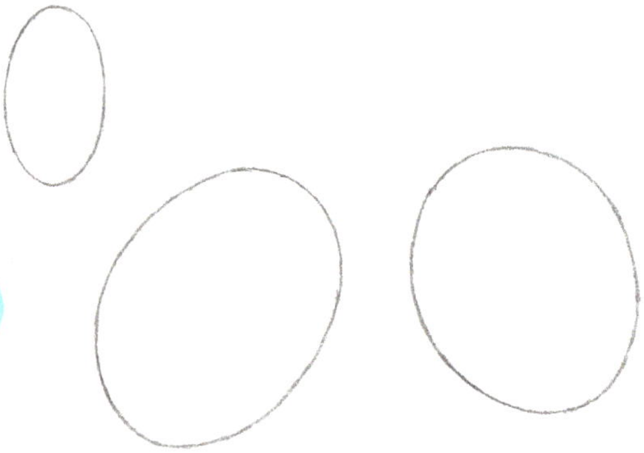

2

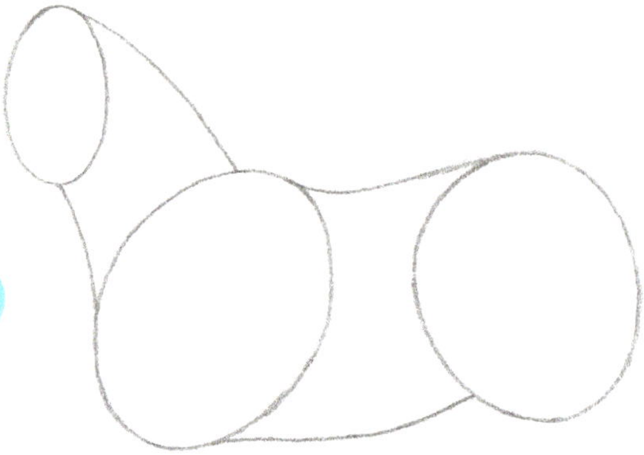

3

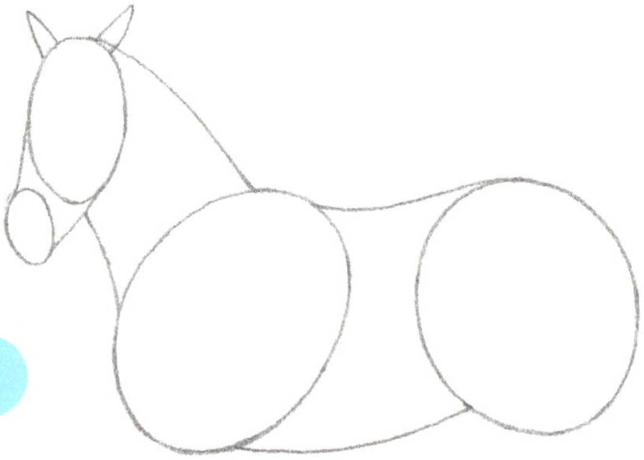

4

fun fact

The first horses in the United States arrived in 1493. By 1780, most Native American tribes had horses, including the Nez Percé of the West. Expert horsemen, the Nez Percé selectively bred spotted horses, which later became the Appaloosa breed.

5

6

7

Percheron

The unfeathered Percheron is a popular heavy breed. Despite its size, it has the elegance of its Arabian ancestors.

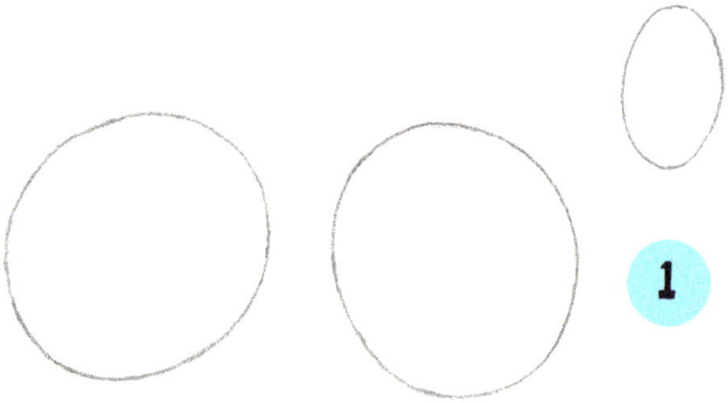

1

2

3

fun fact

Three of the foals recorded in the first American Percheron stud book in 1876 were fathered by a horse named Diligence. Diligence, a native of La Perche, France, arrived in the United States in 1839; once in the states, he reportedly sired more than 400 foals!

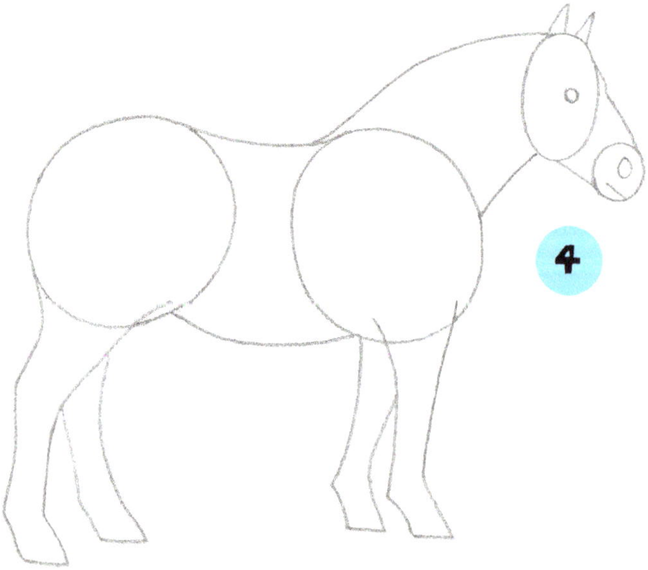

4

5

6

7

Pony of the Americas

This polka-dotted pony has a two-toned mane and a long, arched neck. Draw its spotted coat with circles and ovals.

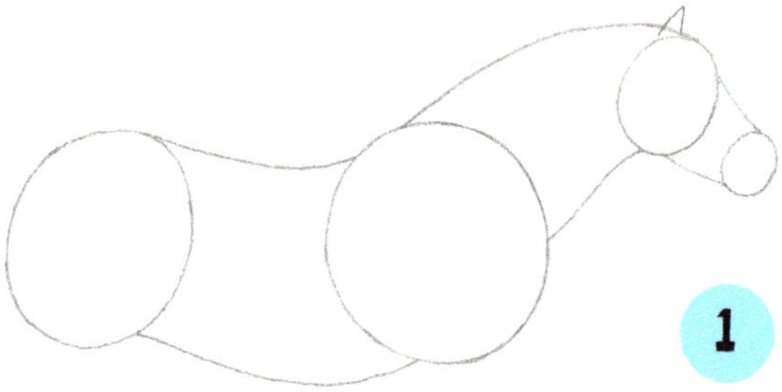

1

2

3

4

fun fact

In 1954, an Iowan breeder named Les Boomhower discovered the unique coat of a foal born with an Arab/Appaloosa mother and a Shetland father. This foal was the first Pony of the Americas, a breed developed for children to show and ride.

5

Tennessee Walking Horse

With its ultra-smooth walk, this gaited horse is a proud show-ring competitor with a sweet, gentle personality.

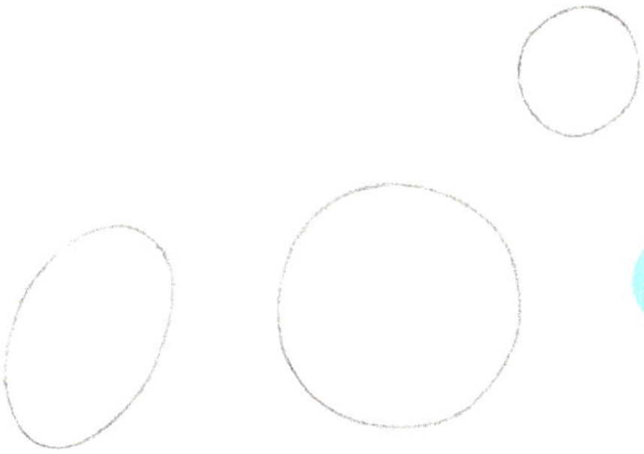

1

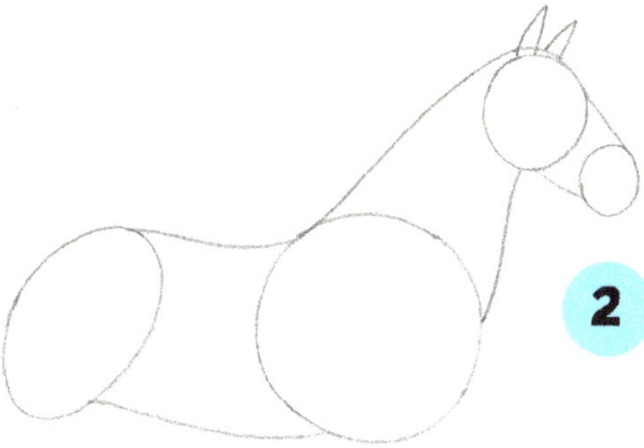

2

3

4

5

6

Dutch Warmblood

Although it's not as tall as its mother, the legs on this athletic foal are already nearly as long and almost as strong as hers!

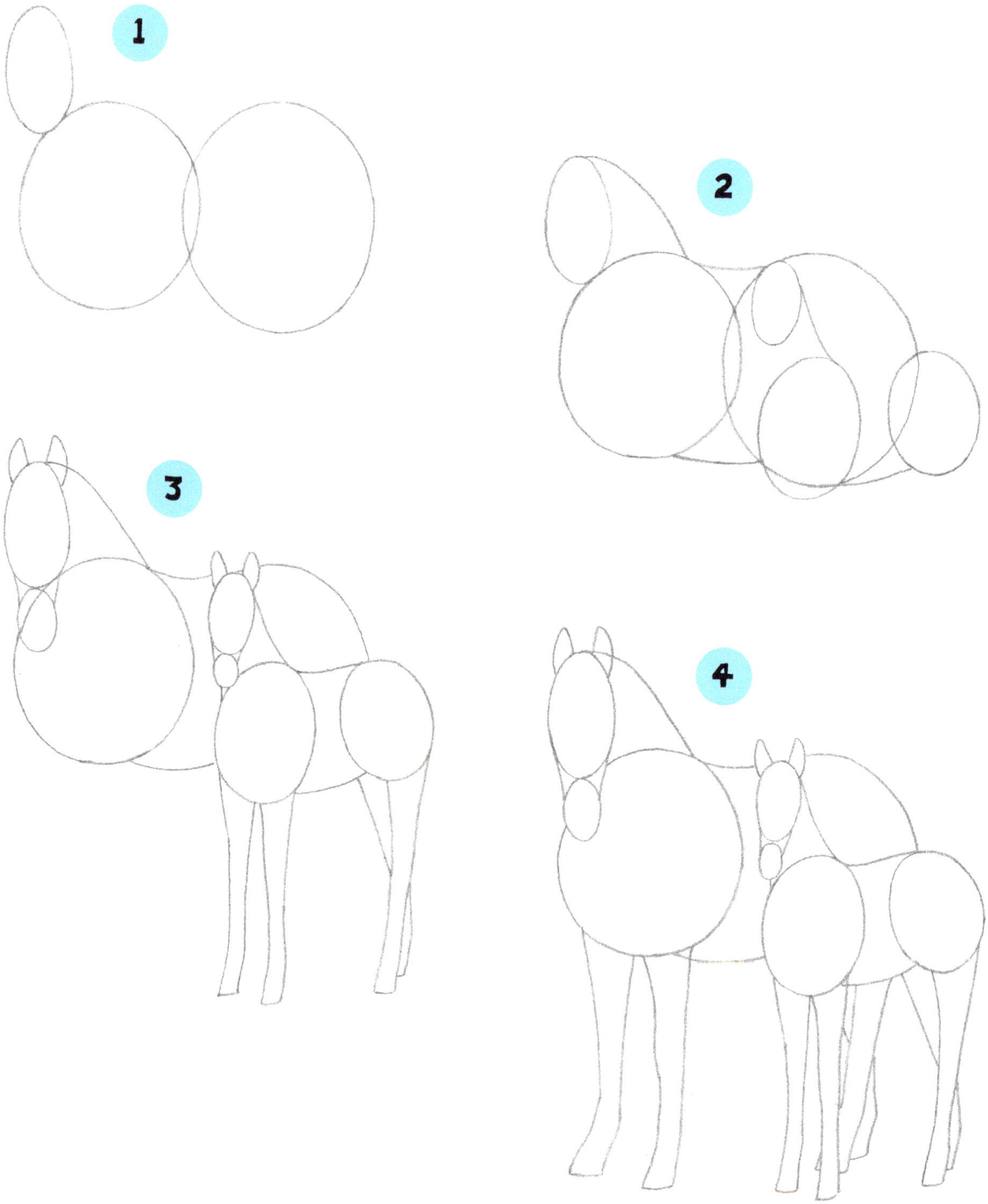

5

6

7

fun fact

Most horses are registered according to their ancestry. For example, if a horse has a registered mother (dam) and father (sire), it's considered to be that breed. But the Dutch Warmblood has an "open" studbook. So regardless of its ancestry, a Dutch Warmblood foal is never automatically accepted for registration. Every foal must first be inspected for breed-worthiness!

Rocky Mountain Pony

Its dappled chocolate coat and creamy mane and tail make this pretty pony a one-of-a-kind sensation!

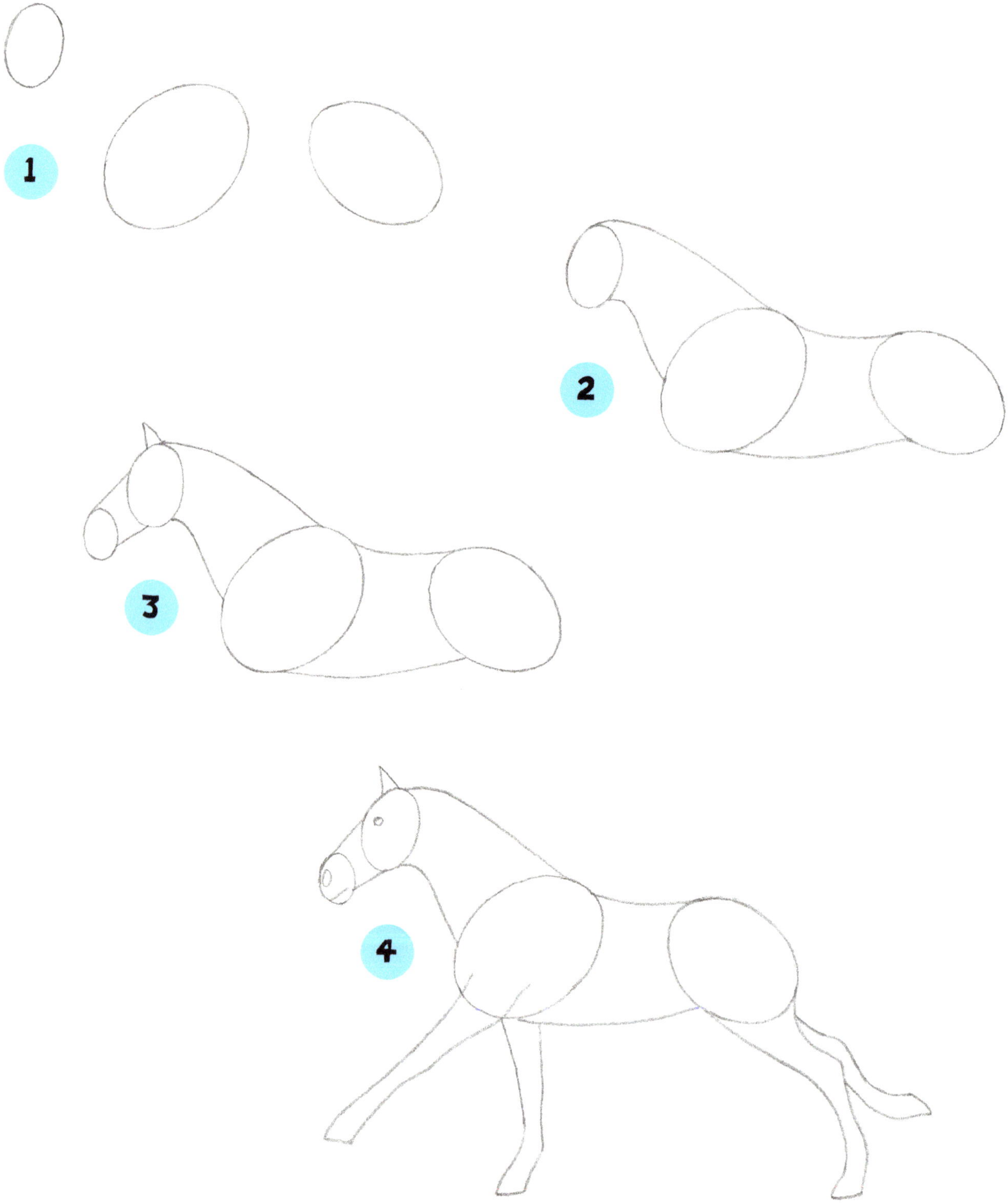

5

6

7

Andalusian

This noble breed is a fabulous gymnast, just like its descendants: the famous "dancing" white Lippizaners of Vienna.

CPSIA information can be obtained
at www.ICGtesting.com
Printed in the USA
BVHW021009111221
623477BV00002B/5

CONTENTS

Introductory Remarks – Beginning with the Character "印" *Yin* (Seal)

1. The character meaning "seal" from the script cut on tortoise shells and bones in ancient China
2. Yuan Dynasty private seal, family name above and signature below —"Wu Signature" (武押)
3. Yuan Dynasty seal, with characters 赵五 reading "Zhao Wu"

The character 印 "*yin*" (seal) is found as early as on the inscriptions on bones and tortoise shells of the Shang Dynasty (1600-1100 BC). It consists of two parts, the top part being the pictograph of a hand and the lower part depicting a kneeling person. The combination of the two parts gives the meaning of "using a hand to press a person downward." Therefore, "pressing down from above" is the usual meaning of the character "*yin*." It was originally a verb, but later became a noun as well.

However, during the period of the Shang and Zhou dynasties some 3,000 years ago, a seal was not called "*yin*," but 玺 "*xi*." But after the First Emperor of the Qin Dynasty (Qin Shihuang) unified China for the first time in history in the year 221 BC, the character 玺 "*xi*" could be used only for the emperor's seal, and all other seals of both the officials at all levels and the common people were called "*yin*." In the Northern Song Dynasty (960-1127), because many people stamped their seals on the paintings and books in their collections, seals were sometimes called "*tushu*," or book. During the Yuan Dynasty (1271-1368), personal signatures tended to replace seals, and therefore seals came to be called "*ya*" or "*huaya*" (both mean signatures).

New names have appeared for the seal one after another since the Han Dynasty (206 BC – 220AD), but "印" and "章 (*zhang*)" have remained the basic names, and therefore "印章" has become a general term.

An emperor's jade seal

The explanation given for "*yin*" in the *Origin of Chinese Characters*, the earliest Chinese dictionary, by Xu Shen (58-147) of the Eastern Han Dynasty, is "government evidence of credibility." As a matter of fact, private seals are also a kind of evidence of credibility. Where the reputation or commitment of an organization or individual was to be proved, the affixing of a symbolic mark was the first function of the seal.

However, if it were only so, seals would not have become a symbol of Chinese culture, because the form of showing reputation or commitment by using seal marks is not peculiar to China. The peculiarity of the Chinese seal lies in the fact that it was a kind of practical article at the beginning, but in the course of its development its function was gradually extended to the field of artistic expression on the basis of practical use. Its carvers changed from ordinary craftsmen to men of letters and artists. It turned from being a mere symbol into a work of art for appreciation. Like Chinese calligraphy, it is based on Chinese characters as the model elements; like Chinese freehand brushwork painting, it values abstract

1. Knob of a jade seal
2. Seal cutting

expression; and like Chinese poems, it lays stress on the artistic conception of beauty. At the same time, seal carving and sculpture are equally excellent, although they are different from each other. Therefore, the seal is a multiple artistic form developed in the nourishment of Chinese arts. The multiplicity of this art is also expressed directly through the seal top engraved in the likeness of an animal, and inscriptions or patterns carved on the sides and top of a seal. In its historical process, the seal has undergone all

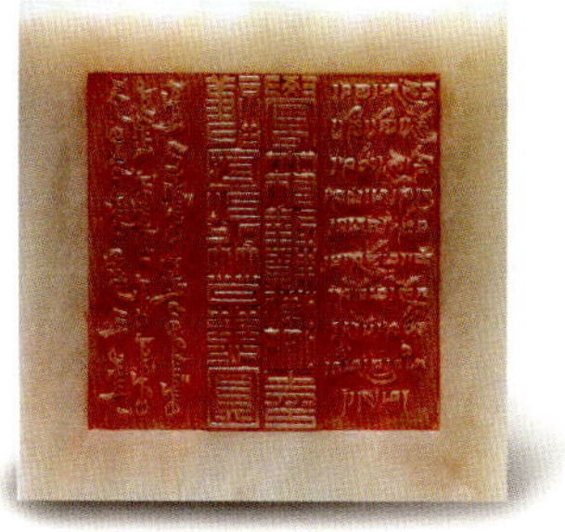

Jade seal bearing inscriptions in the Chinese, Tibetan and Mongolian languages

Large seal with the moon as its theme

kinds of changes in shape, style and taste—from metal casting to stone carving, from stamping in mud to stamping on paper, from the uniformity of the official seals and personal seals to their separation, and from being an article of practical use to being a work of art, and so on. All these changes contain many historical literary allusions. Therefore, the Chinese seal is not only an article for appreciation, it is also an artistic form with profound cultural content, which has kept developing until today through thousands of years. The emblem of the 2008 Beijing Olympic Games is a seal with the Chinese character 京 "*jing*" (capital), which is filled with Chinese traditional cultural flavor and embodies the aesthetics of sport. With this emblem, the Chinese seal shows its peculiar charm to the world.

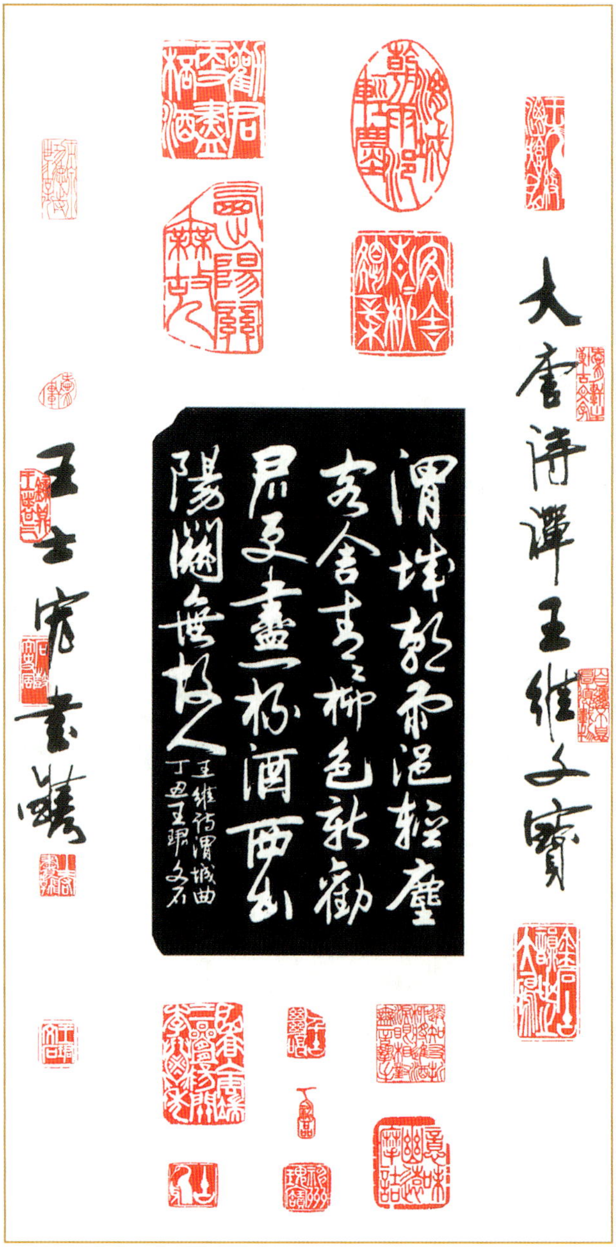

Seal with a poem by Wang Wei

Set of seal carvings with the character 福 (*fu*, or luck)

I

Seals Are Found Everywhere

Seals Stamped on Pottery

Seals Stamped on Clay

Seals Stamped on Paper

Seals on Paintings and Calligraphic Works

The seal is a product of private ownership, and stems from the time man began to have the idea of owning an article for himself. An ancient man stamped a seal on a small ceramic pot on his own behalf one day, and from then on seals have been found everywhere.

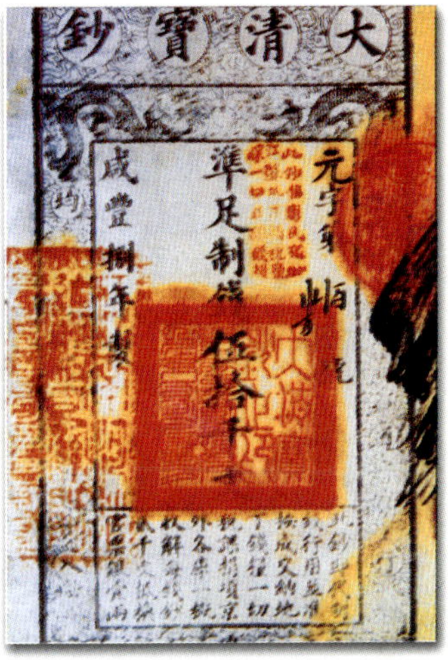

Seal affixed to a Qing Dynasty banknote

Emperors used seals to proclaim their decrees to their people, officials used seals to exercise their power, merchants used seals to demonstrate their credibility, landlords used seals to enclose fields, and the common people used seals to protect their small properties. Gradually, seals became the representative and evidence of personal identity, and even today we are still using seals.

Imperial decree issued by Emperor Shizu of the Qing Dynasty to the Fourth Panchen Lama

Seals Stamped on Pottery

The earliest seal marks were found on pottery. On a piece of broken pottery unearthed in the ruins of Yin, the capital city of the late Shang Dynasty in Anyang, Henan Province, were found raised characters, showing that there was already something similar to a seal in the Shang Dynasty. It was stamped on the surface of the pot as a certain kind of symbol. In both its use and its symbolic function was very close to those of the seals of later days. The stamping of seals on items of pottery became very common in the Spring and Autumn and Warring States (770 BC – 221 BC) periods. The sizes of the seals were often determined

1. Sealed pottery of the Warring States Period
2. The character "关" (pass) carved on an eave tile
3. Imperial decree sealed on ceramic ware of the Qin Dynasty

according to the sizes of the pottery items. The stamp mainly indicated the names of the workshops and craftsmen involved in the making of the piece. This was known as "stamped pottery." After Qin Shihuang united China, imperial decrees issued on uniform weights and measures were either engraved directly on a bronze weight or carved on seals and stamped on pottery. Stamped pottery became a kind of government announcement.

1
2
3
4

1. Sealed clay of the Warring States Period
2. Seal stamped on clay
3. Sealed clay, Han Dynasty. The inscription "平原大尹章" (*ping yuan da yin zhang*) means "Seal of the prefect of Pingyuan."
4. The informal inscription on this seal, "可以清心也" (*ke yi qing xin ye*) means "Be carefree."

Seals Stamped on Clay

During the Spring and Autumn and Warring States periods, seals were stamped on the clay used to seal letters and other items wrapped and dispatched. Sticky clay was smeared over the knot of the cotton rope used to tie the parcel, and the seal was affixed to this. This was supposed to prevent the package being opened by unauthorized persons.

When a letter was wrapped and sealed, a piece of wood would be added on the bamboo or wood slips on which a letter was written. It was called 检 (*jian*),

and was equivalent to the label in the later days. The wood was carved with a square hole where a knot was made of the rope tying the letter. The knot was sealed with clay on which the seal was affixed.

So far, more than 700 pieces of stamped sealing clay dating from the Han Dynasty have been found in Shaanxi and Shandong provinces.

The seal marks on the sealing clay as a whole bear the names of persons. Seals of officials usually bear their titles, such as

1 2
3 4
5

1. Slang and pithy remarks were also used in seal inscriptions.

2. The inscription on this seal, "出入大吉" (*chu ru da ji*) means "Good luck coming and going."

3. The palindromic inscription on this seal, "言顾行，行顾言" (*yan gu xing, xing gu yan*) means "*Making good on your promise*."

4. The inscription on this seal, "日利" (*ri li*) means "Prosper day by day."

5. Seal (representing the authority of the God or the Heavenly Master), used by Taoist masters at rites to summon wind, rain or gods, or dispel evils and comfort the souls of the dead.

sima (minister of war), *sigong* (minister of works) and *silu* (minister of finance). Common people often had their names carved in different sizes and shapes of seals—square, round, triangular or heart-shaped. Sometimes, there were seals in the shape of objects in daily life. The most common of these were those in the shape of animals, including the 12 animals (rat, ox, tiger, rabbit, dragon, snake, horse, sheep, monkey, rooster, dog and pig), representing the 12 Earthly Branches, used to symbolize the year in which a person is born. But there were also exotic animals such as the ostrich and rhinoceros, which were rare in China. Such seals were very popular during the Warring States period and the Han Dynasty. They were not only used for identification, but also used as talismans to ward off evil spirits and bring good luck. There were also seals bearing auspicious phrases. *Chang* (prosperity) and *zheng xing* (honorable conduct) were popular in the Warring

1 2
3

1. Seal portraying a man riding a tiger, indicating the achievement of immortality
2. Seal bearing a likeness of Dijun, a deity of the ancient Yin ethnic group. The god has a bird's head and a bear's body. It is believed that the seal can bring good luck and expel evil spirits.
3. Heavenly Master's seal

1 2

1. Seal with the inscription "宜子孙" (*yi zi sun*, or Good for children). It was used as a talisman by people who wished for increased progeny.
2. Portrait seal showing a servant ready to water exotic flowers planted in pots under the guidance of his master

States Period, and *he zhong* (harmonious crowd) and *jing shi* (handling matters cautiously) in the Qin Dynasty. Later, Taoists carved *huang shen yue zhang* and *tian di shen shi* (Divine Master of Heaven and Earth) on their seals. They believed the seals can drive away ferocious beasts and evil spirits and used them as religious instruments.

Seals Stamped on Paper

Although paper of considerable good quality was made in 105 in the Eastern Han Dynasty, it was not widely used in day-to-day affairs until the Southern and Northern Dynasties (420-589), when it replaced bamboo and wooden slips as the medium for writing. As a result, sealing clay was gradually abandoned, as seals were stamped on paper

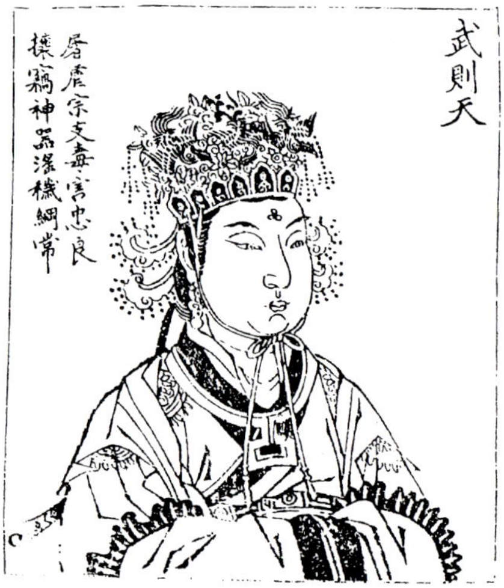

Believing that the characters "玺" (*xi*, or imperial seal) and "死" (*si*, meaning death) were homophones, Empress Wu Zetian of the Tang Dynasty decided to change "玺" (*xi*) to "宝" (*bao*) as the word for seal.

instead of on clay. According to the *Annals of Northern Qi*, red ink was used for seals in the reign of Emperor Wu of the Liang Dynasty (502-557). Black and red seal marks can be seen on the model calligraphic works and paintings passed down from the Southern Qi (479-502) and Tang (618-907) dynasties as well as on ancient documents unearthed in the Xinjiang Uygur Autonomous Region.

When seals began to be stamped on paper, the form of the seal marks changed. Previously, because the seals were stamped on clay, the characters on the seals were cut in intaglio, so that the characters on the clay emerged in relief, clearly recognizable. When the seals were stamped on paper, it was necessary to distinguish the marks by some other means. Therefore, from the Sui Dynasty (581-618) on, the marks on the seals were cut in relief, and stamped on a pad of red—and, less frequently, black—ink before being transferred to the paper.

From then on, red seals were found on all kinds of papers—imperial decrees, official pronouncements, and contracts and letters exchanged among merchants.

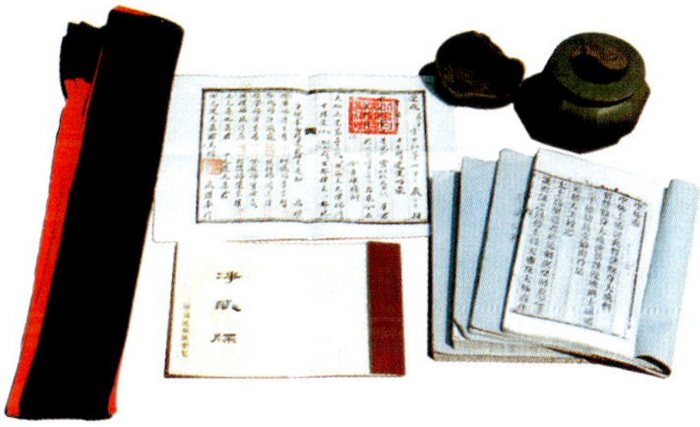

1. Seal cut by Xi Gang, one of the "Eight Masters of Xiling"
2. Seal cut by Chen Yuzhong, one of the "Eight Masters of Xiling"
3. Taoist ordination certificate with an official seal

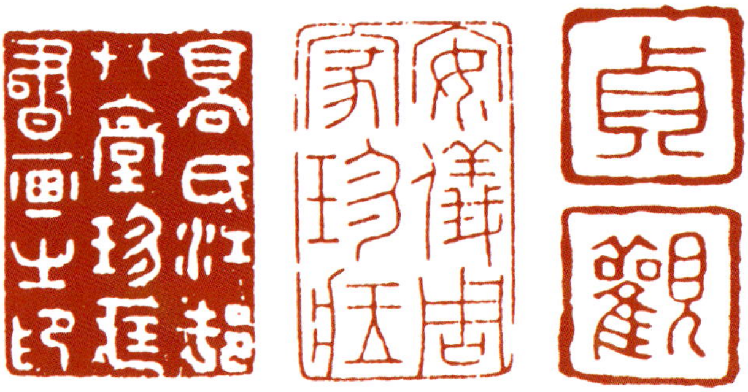

1 2 3

1. Seal of admiration and collection
2. Seal of admiration and collection
3. "贞观" (Zhenguan) reign title seal of Emperor Taizong of the Tang Dynasty

Seals on Paintings and Calligraphic Works

During the Sui and Tang dynasties collecting calligraphic works and paintings by public organizations and individuals came into vogue, and the collectors became accustomed to applying their personal seals to these works.

There were two kinds of such seals: One was the seal of the creator, and the other was the seal of the collector (or in some cases a seal applied by a distinguished connoisseur to show his appreciation). Almost all collection and appreciation seals

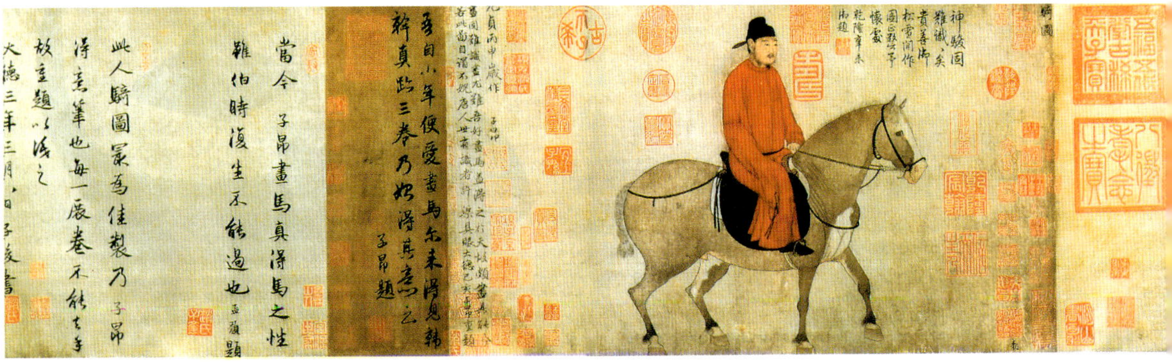

A painting by Zhao Mengfu, a calligrapher and painter of the Yuan Dynasty, *Man Riding a Horse*. It bears the seals of collectors of later periods. The biggest number of seals are those of the Qing Emperor Qianlong.

during the Eastern Jin Dynasty (317-420) were simply personal seals. The "Zhenguan" (627-650) reign title seal of Emperor Taizong and the "Kaiyuan" (713-742) reign title seal of Emperor Xuanzong, both of the Tang Dynasty, are the earliest such seals extant. During the subsequent Five Dynasties (907-960) and the two Song Dynasties (960-1279), the imperial families were all avid collectors of paintings and calligraphic works, and never failed to stamp their reign titles on their treasures. Sometimes the seals of government departments are found on such works. In the Southern Song Dynasty (1127-1279) more and more individuals collected calligraphic works and paintings, and the seals for collection and appreciation were in multifarious forms. For example, added under the personal names or the names of libraries were such combinations of characters as 收藏 *shou cang* (collected), 考藏 *kao cang* (collected after textual research), 珍藏 *zhen cang* (treasured and collected), 鉴藏 *jian cang* (admired and collected), 藏画 *cang hua* (collected painting), 珍玩 *zhen wan* (curio), 秘玩 *mi wan* (private curio), 珍秘 *zhen mi* (treasured curio), 鉴赏 *jian shang* (appreciated), 清赏 *qing shang* (elegant object for refined enjoyment), 心赏 *xin shang* (elegant object for visual enjoyment) and 过眼 *guo yan* (glanced at).

1. Seal of admiration and collection, with the characters "图籍" (Map of territory and register of population)
2. Seal of admiration and collection, with the characters "鉴赏" (appreciation)

Similar seals are found on treasured books. Often added under the personal name of the collector or the name of the library where the book is stored are such combinations of characters as 藏书印 *cang shu yin* (collected book seal), 图书之记 *tu shu zhi ji* (book seal) and 图籍印 *tu ji yin* (manuscript seal).

Seals of creators of calligraphic works and paintings earlier than the Tang Dynasty have not been found. During the Northern Song Dynasty (960–1127), Ouyang Xiu, Wen Tong, Su Shi, Mi Fu and other great calligraphers and painters used their seals on letters occasionally. However, calligraphers and painters of the Yuan (1206-1368) and succeeding dynasties always stamped their seals on their works. The seals carried the name and alias of the artist, and sometimes his birthplace.

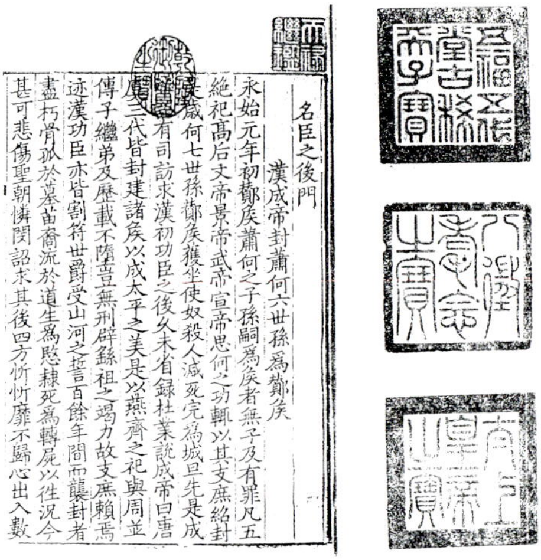

Book collector's seals with the characters "太上皇帝之宝" (*tai shang huang di zhi bao*, or Supreme Emperor's Treasure) and "乾隆御览" (*qian long yu lan*, or Book for Emperor Qianlong's Reading)

Other seals applied to calligraphic works and paintings bore such characters as 某某斋 (a certain study), 某某堂 (a certain hall), 某某馆 (a certain house) or 某某阁 (a certain pavilion). Such seals were also called *zhai tang guan ge* seals (seals for study, hall, house and pavilion). 端居室 *duan ju shi* (leisure time studio) was the inscription on the seal of Li Mi, a prime minister in the Tang Dynasty. This was the earliest "study, hall, house and pavilion" seal, and is recorded in the *Collection of Ancient Seals* by Gan Yang of the Ming Dynasty (1368-1644). Later, many men of letters gave elegant names to their own residences, and had these names carved on their seals. However, these names sometimes did not represent actual buildings, but only conveyed their owners' aspirations.

Li Mi's "study and hall" seal, with the characters "端居室" (*duan ju shi*)

Moreover, seals stamped on calligraphic works and paintings also include such phrases as 引首章 *yin shou zhang* (foremost seal) and 押角章 *ya jiao zhang* (bottom corner seal). They identify the part of the work where the seal should be stamped.

The "foremost" seals were stamped on the upper right-hand corner of the work. They are also called 迎首章 (leading seal). The inscription on such a seal was usually an elegant phrase or the name of a studio or house. Different from the personal name seals, which are generally square, the "foremost" seals are usually oblong.

The seal stamped on the bottom corner of a work carried the same inscription as the "foremost" seals, but were generally square. It served the function of marking the boundary of a work, so that when it was mounted, no part of the work within the corner seal would be excised.

The use of seals on paintings and calligraphic works is a peculiar characteristic of Chinese seals. Such seals became an art in themselves.

Painting by Wen Zhengming – *Mountain Trees in a Spring Mist*

Painting by Wu Changshuo – *Monk with a Sack* (1914)

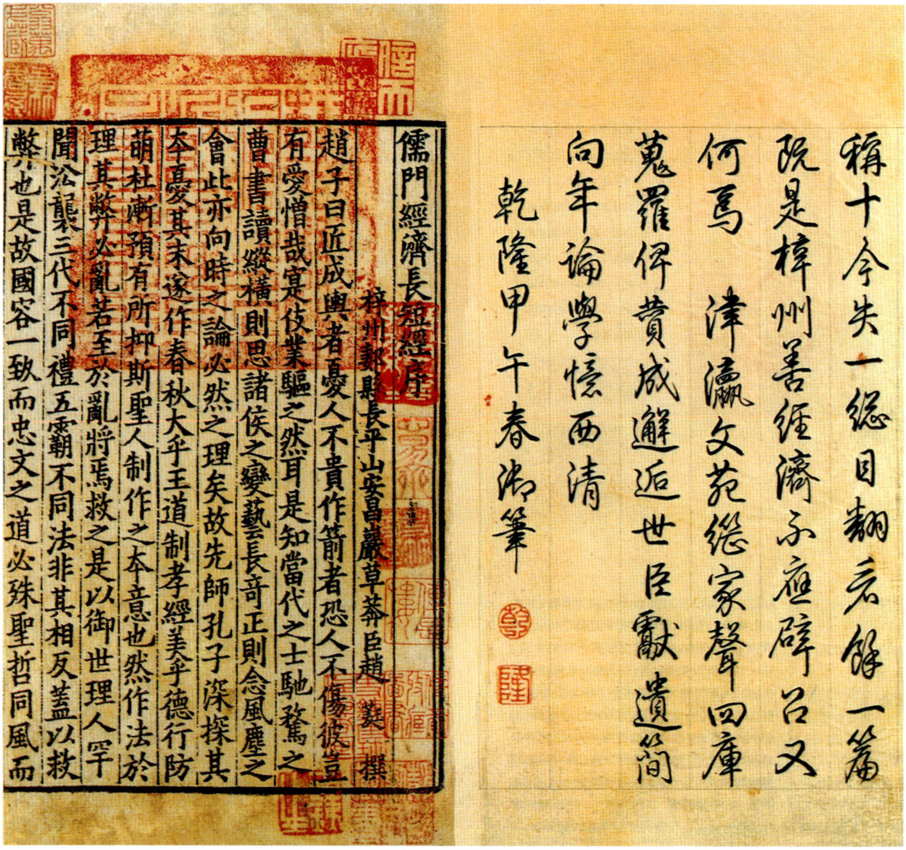

Block-printed edition of the *Classic of Long and Short Scriptures* of the Northern Song Dynasty. On the right is an inscription by Emperor Qianlong of the Qing Dynasty, below which are two seals. The round one bears the character "乾" (*qian*), and the square one the character "隆" (*long*). On the left side on the top of the book cover is a large imperial seal; the others are mostly collectors' seals.

II

The Historical Development of Chinese Seals

The Earliest Seals

Seals of the Spring and Autumn and Warring States Periods

Qin and Han Dynasty Seals, and Their Decline

Separation of Official Seals and Private Seals, and the Appearance of the Art of Seal Cutting

The Earliest Seals

China's earliest seal dates back to the Shang Dynasty. It is a fragment of pottery unearthed in the ruins of that dynasty in Anyang, Henan Province, as mentioned above. The piece is only half of a square seal, and was verified as a seal when three small similar seals of bronze were found in the 1930s. The inscriptions on all these seals are cut in relief.

Seals of the Spring and Autumn and Warring States Periods

During the Spring and Autumn and Warring States periods (722-221 BC), treaties and agreements between the various states, which were constantly at war with each other, called for ratification and guarantees, and these were provided by means of seals. It became the custom to issue a seal to a newly appointed official. At the same time, traders clinched business deals with

1 2 3

1. Ancient seal of the Warring States Period, bearing the characters "康都右司马" (*kang du you si ma*, or Right Minister of War for Kangdu)
2. Appeal and response in seal characters
3. A private seal of the Warring States Period. It is also called a "small seal." The characters on it read "周常" (*zhou chang*), a name.

seals. Both the official and individual seals were called 玺 (*xi*) . This was the first period of development of Chinese seals.

Chiseled seal "振威将军章" (*zhen wei jiang jun zhang*, or Power-spreading General's seal)

During the Warring States Period (475-221 BC), China already boasted a mature bronze casting industry, thus enabling the casting of bronze seals. Some had inscriptions engraved on the faces of the cast bronze pieces, but most seals were cast with the inscriptions already on them.

Qin and Han Dynasty Seals, and Their Decline

After Emperor Qin Shihuang unified China in 221 BC, he adopted a series of policies and measures to consolidate his rule. As mentioned above, henceforth only the emperor's seal was called a 玺 *xi*, while the seals of the officials and common people were called 印 *yin*. Moreover, there were also strictly graded differences in the seals for different classes of people, including different types of handles and strings for attaching the seals to belts, etc.

Mount Tai stone carving, Qin Dynasty, with seal characters in the *xiaozhuan* style

The Han Dynasty inherited the

1 2 3

1. Official seal of the Qin Dynasty
2. Seal of the Han Dynasty, "上将军印章" (*shang jiang jun yin zhang*, or Senior General's Seal)
3. Official seal of the Han Dynasty. The inscription "假司马印" (*jia si ma yin*) means "Seal of the Deputy War Minister."

institutions of the Qin Dynasty, and for many years in the early period of the Western Han Dynasty (206 BC-8 AD), the seal regulations followed the practice established in the Qin Dynasty. In the first year of his reign (104 BC), Emperor Wu ordered that the seals used by officials should respectively be called 章 *zhang* or 印 *yin*, depending on their official ranks, while private seals had to bear the two additional characters 私印 *si yin* (private seal) following the seal owner's name. At the same time, the material of the seal, the shape of its handle and the color of the silk string were different, corresponding to the different official ranks. The shapes of the seals were all uniform, almost invariably square.

This system survived intact until the period of the Three Kingdoms (220-265), when chronic turbulence led to the downfall of officials in rapid succession, and the hasty appointment of new ones. As there was little time in those conditions for the casting of new seals, the measure adopted was to cast a large number of seals with

General's seal

blank faces for reserve, and have them cut whenever an official was appointed. This practice led to a relaxing of the strict protocol which had governed seal making since Qin times.

During the Southern and Northern Dynasties, the regulations relating to seals were virtually abandoned. Seals gradually became larger, and the technique of cutting inscriptions in relief emerged. Rules dictating the dimensions and nature of the inscriptions on seals did not reappear until the Ming Dynasty (1368-1644), under the influence of men of letters and seal cutters.

Separation of Official Seals and Private Seals, and the Appearance of the Art of Seal Cutting

Seals were divided into "official seals" and "private seals" as early as the Spring and Autumn Period because of their uses on different occasions. The official seals were used for the exercise of political power and functions, while the private seals were used for associations and contacts among the members of society as evidence

1 2 3

1. Official seal of the Warring States Period. It is about one and half inches high.
2. A private seal of the Warring States Period
3. Official seal of the Sui Dynasty. The inscription "观阳县印" (*guan yang xian yin*) means "Guanyang County Seal."

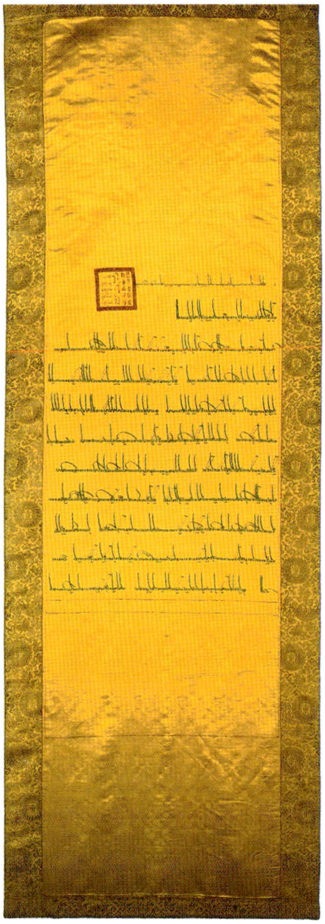

1. Gold seal issued by Emperor Yongzheng of the Qing Dynasty to the seventh Dalai Lama
2. Imperial decree issued by Emperor Kangxi of the Qing Dynasty conferring the title of the fifth Panchen Lama. The emperor's jade seal bears inscriptions in the Manchu, Chinese and Tibetan languages.

of trustworthiness. However, there was not much difference in the basic shape and structure of the two types. Beginning in the Sui Dynasty (581-618), the difference between the official seals and private seals in the shape and structure became gradually clear. The main manifestation was that the official seals became larger, while the private seals remained unchanged. In the Tang Dynasty (618-907), the official seals and the private seals became even more differentiated. In 1012 during the Northern Song Dynasty, the government issued orders to prohibit the casting of private seals. Henceforth, private seals could only be made of wood or bone.

With the further development of calligraphy and painting in the Tang and Song dynasties, many calligraphers and painters began to stamp their seals on their works as evidence that they were the creators. Therefore,

1. Eight-faced seal

2. A set of seals

dynasties, human figures as well as those of animals appeared as decorations for the knobs of private seals. However, they can hardly be compared with those of the Han Dynasty for richness of artistry and elegance.

A further development in seal-cutting art came about when artisans discovered certain types of stone which lent themselves better to carving than the traditional materials. The reigns of emperors Kangxi and Qianlong of the Qing Dynasty (the end of the 17th century to the end of the 18th century) saw the peak of the development of the seal knob art in China, and many seal knob cutting masters emerged. The Qing emperors demanded valuable stone seals as part of the annual tribute delivered to them by their vassals, and employed master craftsmen to make exquisite seals with elaborate knobs for the imperial seals. Seal knob cutting masters commemorated in historical records include Yang Yuxuan of the Kangxi reign period, and Zhou Shangjun of the Qianlong reign period, both "imperial craftsmen" at their respective courts. Many stone seal knobs cut by famous masters were owned by

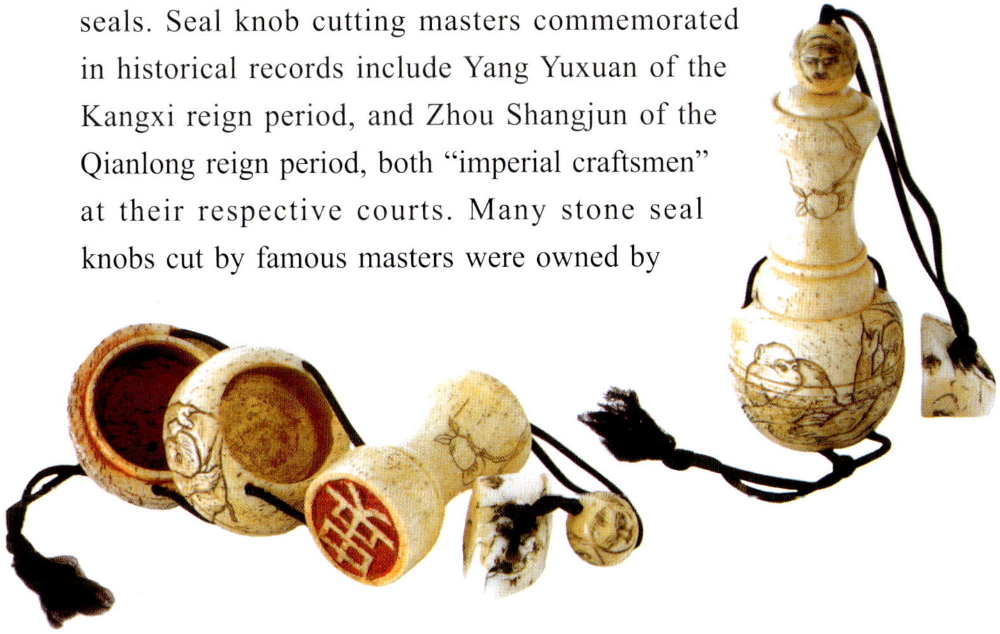

Seal knob in the shape of a lion

emperors and their relatives, and a large number of these are in the Palace Museum collection.

During the Ming and Qing dynasties, the achievements made in seal knob art can be said to be a miniature record of the 5,000-year-old Chinese art of stone carving. This is because they not only make full use of the technique of expression in the plastic art of stone carving, such as sculpture-in-the-round, relief, fretwork, intaglio and concave cutting, they also combine carving, calligraphy and painting into one in a "square inch of space" with all kinds of exquisite shapes and postures, creating a unique artistic world.

The seal knobs were carved into the shapes of animals, flowers, plants, mountains, rivers, trees, rocks, pavilions, towers, human figures, fruits and vegetables. In addition, there were also imitations of ancient objects or patterns on ancient objects, including the dragon and butterfly design commonly seen on jade objects and the *taotie* (a mythical animal) design commonly seen on bronze ware. Such seal knobs were called *bo gu niu* (imitation antique knob). Just like ordinary jade carving, seal knob cutting stresses *qiao se* (skill and color), i.e. the skilful use of the

Seal knob

natural colors, quality, forms and grains of the seal stones, and regards them as an organic part of the carving, thus achieving the perfect unity of Nature and artisanship.

In addition, there was something called *bo yi* (faint concept), which refers to carvings in low relief around the surface of a stone seal. This had the same decorative flavor as that of the seal knob. As it uses a very low relief to create the sentiment normally created by a poem or painting, it is called "faint concept." This cutting technique was first used by Yang Yuxuan and Zhou Shangjun of the Qing Dynasty. Its modeling and composition were both based on the shape, color and grain of the stone used. A shallow outline was cut, and subtle gradations scraped with a graver, thus forming an abstruse tableau. This technique relies on simplicity and brevity for its success. Its main subjects include figures, landscapes, pavilions, clouds, the moon, flowers, birds, insects and fish. In the late Qing Dynasty, historical episodes were also used as subjects, including *chibi huaigu* (Reflections on the Red Cliff), *zhulin qixian* (The Seven Sages of the Bamboo Grove) and *huxi sanxiao* (The Tiger Roars Thrice).

Side carving

Seal knob

"Reflections on the Red Cliff" is based on a poem by Su Shi of the Song Dynasty. The poem conveys the writer's feelings about a famous battle in the Three Kingdoms period. It was a battle in which a weak force defeated a much stronger one.

"The Seven Sages of the Bamboo Grove" were seven men of letters during the Three Kingdoms period who gathered in a bamboo grove to chant poems, drink wine and play the zither.

"The Tiger Roars Thrice": During the Eastern Jin Dynasty, a Buddhist scholar called Hui Yuan lived in the Donglin Temple on Mount Lushan, having vowed that he would not leave it for 30 years. There was a brook by the temple. If he crossed the brook, a tiger would roar. One day, the poet Tao Yuanming paid Hui Yuan a visit. As they walked and chatted happily, they crossed the brook without knowing it. Hui Yuan did not realize that he had done so until the tiger had roared three times.

IV

The Story of Seal Stones

During the Yuan Dynasty, calligraphers and painters began to take part in the creation of seals. At that time, seals were still made by craftsmen, with the men of letters designing the inscriptions. Then a painter called Wang Mian (1287-1359), who was famous for depicting plum blossoms, took an interest in seal cutting. He found that most of the materials used for seals at that time were bronze, jade and ivory—all of hard texture. These materials were not only comparatively rare, but hard to cut. While walking near his native village by Mount Baohua in Tiantai, Lishui County, Zhejiang Province, he discovered by chance a smooth stone called *huayao shi* (anther stone), which was soft and easy to carve. It was not necessary to be a skilled craftsman to

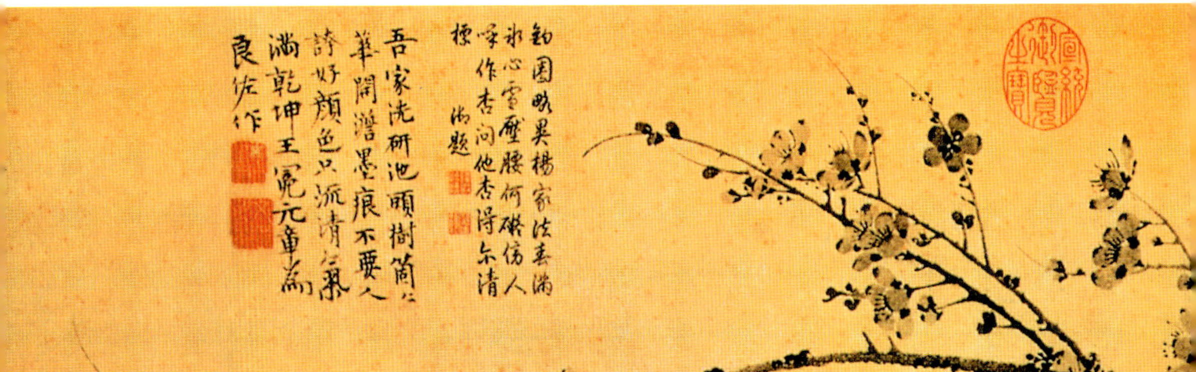

Painting of plum blossoms by Wang Mian

carve on it, and so it came about that scholars themselves started to carve their own seals.

The types of stone most commonly used for seal engraving are Shoushan stone (agalmatolite), Qingtian stone, Changhua stone and Balin stone. Each has its own texture, color and other properties.

Shoushan stone, which is also called *hushi* (kettle stone) or *tashi* (tower stone), is found in the Shoushan area, 40 km north of the city of Fuzhou in eastern China's Fujian Province. It is a secondary mineral, which formed after alteration from magnesium silicate. It is glossy and wax-like. It comes in light yellow, brown and green colors, and is classified into three categories, according to the three different places of its origin: *tiankeng* (field pit stone), *shuikeng* (water pit stone) and *shankeng* (mountain pit stone). Field pit stone is found in an ancient sand layer under the paddy fields along the two sides of a stream winding several km through Shoushan Township. The most precious *tianhuang* stone, whose value equals that of gold of the same weight, is found here. Of the water pit stone types, the *shuijingdong* (crystal jelly), (the transparent body of the seal stones looks similar to the jelly and is therefore called "jelly"), *yunaodong* (fish brain jelly), *dongyoushi* (frozen oil stone), *huangdong* (yellow jelly), *shancaodong* (eel weeds jelly), *taohuadong* (the peach blossom jelly), *manaodong* (agate jelly) and *huandong* (ring jelly) are all well known.

Qingtian stone is found about 10 km outside the Qingtian County town, Zhejiang Province. It is similar to Shoushan stone in structure and hardness. This stone is normally found among large areas of rough rocks and the size of the raw stone is not big. It was first mined in the Song Dynasty for carving into small utensils. Wen Peng of the Ming Dynasty was the first to use lamplight jelly stone for cutting seals. Many men of letters and seal cutters followed suit, making it really popular. Generally Qingtian stone has a fine and compact texture and rich luster. Its colors include white, yellow, red, light green, dark green, grey, dark reddish brown and black. The light green is the most common. Its main products include *dengguangdong* (lamplight jelly, as it is pure, fine and smooth, and with excellent transparency against the lamplight), *yunaodong* (fish brain jelly), *baiguodong* (ginkgo jelly), *jiangyoudong* (soy sauce jelly) and *zitandong* (sandalwood jelly).

Seal stones

Changhua stone is found in Changhua County, Zhejiang Province. This type of stone is divided into wet pit and dry pit varieties. Wet pit stone has an even texture, while dry pit stone is coarse and hard. It occurs in red, yellow and grey colors, which are often mixed together. One variety is known as *oufendong* (lotus root jelly, or Changhua jelly), as it looks like cooked lotus root starch jelly, and is considered of the best quality. Another is called *jixueshi* (chicken blood stone), because it contains substances the color of chicken blood. If a stone has the three colors of black, white and red it is called *Liuguanzhang* (i.e. Liu Bei, Guan Yu and Zhang Fei, the principal heroes in the classical novel *Romance of the Three Kingdoms*). If a stone is fully covered with "chicken blood," it enjoys the reputation of *dahongpao* (bright red gown), and is regarded as the rarest and most precious of the soft stone varieties.

Balin stone is found in the area of Mount Yamatu in the Balin Right Banner, Zhaowuda League, Inner Mongolia Autonomous Region. It is a type of pyrophyllite, and has been mined in North China only since 1973.

The literati gave the seal stones "six virtues": *xi* (fine), *jie* (knotty), *run* (smooth), *ni* (delicate), *wen* (warm) and *ning* (congealing). A precious stone seal not only has the value of the seal, but also high aesthetic and artistic value for the stone itself. Since ancient times, there has been a saying: "Once you have a seal, you'll live as long as metal and stone." Therefore, many

Seal stones

people collect valuable seal stones. The stone lovers keep them in embroidered boxes, wrapped in brocade. Sometimes, they also apply tea oil or walnut oil to increase the luster of the stones. As time goes by, the seal stones become warmer and smoother, and as the owners caress them, the stones are gradually imbued with the warmth of their hands. The longer the stones are kept, the purer and better is their ancient natural luster.

Seal stone in an embroidered box

V

The Beauty of the Seal Characters and Seal Style

Seal cutting

The quintessence of the beauty of Chinese seals lies in the skilful combination of the vivid shapes of the Chinese characters, the harmonious seal face composition and the cutting technique. The different lines, shapes and seal face layouts all have historical antecedents.

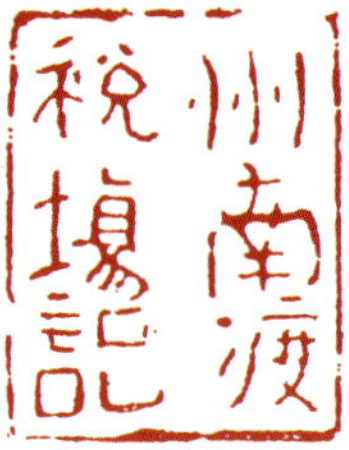

1. Seal cut in the regular script. The characters read "州南渡税场记" (*zhou nan du shui chang ji*, or Zhounandu Tax Office).
2. *Dazhuan*, ancient style of calligraphy used on seals of the Warring States Period

Seal Inscriptions

The Chinese characters inscribed on seals are special in that the carver has to strive for harmony, proper balance and orderly arrangement of the strokes. Several styles of calligraphy were used for seal inscriptions down the ages.

Seal with a poem by Li Bai

Dazhuan 大篆 is a style of calligraphy developed in the Zhou Dynasty and used up until the Qin Dynasty. The various states into which China was divided in those days used different versions of this script. It is an ancient style featuring free-flowing and gentle strokes. It is an unrestrained and natural style.

Xiaozhuan 小篆 was adopted in the Qin Dynasty.

After the First Emperor of the Qin Dynasty unified China, he ordered his prime minister, Li Si, to compile a list of standard characters for use in writing all over the new empire. The *xiaozhuan* script which Li Si devised was simpler than the *dazhuan* in structure, the thickness of the strokes was well-balanced, the turns of the strokes were smoother and more fluent, and the shape and structure were even and symmetrical. As this style took shape in the Qin Dynasty, it is also called *Qin zhuan*.

Moyin Style 摹印体

This style evolved on the basis of the *xiaozhuan*, as a special

1 2 3

1. "Bird-and-insect" *zhuan* style of calligraphy. The characters read "武意" (*wu yi*, or military will).
2. Suspended needle characters
3. Suspended needle characters cut in the *zhuan* style

script used for seal cutting in the Qin Dynasty. It was the standard script for official seals at that time. It changed the round turn of the *xiaozhuan* into a square or circle, and increased or decreased the number of strokes in a character, mainly to meet the requirements of the layouts on the square seal faces. This style was not widely used for seals until the mid- and late-Western Han Dynasty, and is sometimes called *Han zhuan*.

Mouzhuan 缪篆

A variant of the *moyin* style, this method of writing tended to bend or extend characters for the purpose of filling the seal face. 缪 *mou* means twisting or winding.

Jiudie (nine folds) characters

Bird and Insect Characters 鸟虫书

This is a decorative seal character style. Its strokes are reminiscent of the shapes of birds and insects. It was popular in Han times.

Suspended Needle Characters 悬针书

This style was popular during the Three Kingdoms period. It prolongs the vertical strokes of the *mouzhuan* character and ends them with a needle-like point. This style leaves the characters without a cohesive force among the strokes. It is a weak style in contrast to the powerfulness and simplicity of the seal styles used in the Qin and Han dynasties.

Jiudie (nine folds) Writing 九叠文

Seal faces were enlarged during the Tang and Song dynasties. In order to fill up the extra space on the seal face, the strokes of the characters forming the inscriptions were wound and coiled. *jiu* (nine) means "too many" here, not necessarily "nine." This style was used throughout the Yuan, Ming and Qing dynasties for official seals, and was not abandoned until the end of the dynastic period in the early 20th century.

The Composition of Seal Inscriptions

A seal combining skillfulness and "clumsiness"

The two basic rules of seal inscription cutting are, first, that there should be no erroneous strokes in the characters used in the inscription, and, two, that character styles should not be mixed.

Seal inscriptions nearly always feature one or the other of the special seal character styles, called 篆法 (seal character writing technique). It was not merely a mechanical copy of the metal and stone characters of ancient times, but writing with originality for the different forms of seals, different relationships between character and character, and different artistic conceptions of the seals. In this respect, the "mood" and "linear beauty" were what the seal cutters took pains to depict.

The so-called "mood" conveyed in the seal characters is one in which the "cut" characters convey the same flavor as calligraphic characters in terms of quickness, slowness, lightness, heaviness.

Seal cutters often talk about "brush strokes" and "depth of ink," just as calligraphers do.

Moreover, just as a painter executes a painting, seal cutters pay attention to brief and solemn straight lines, mild, fluent and beautiful curves, calm and broad lateral lines, dynamic and thrilling diagonal lines, majestic and powerful bold lines, and slender and vigorous thin lines. Just like famous painters, leading seal cutters are known for their professional technique; for instance, Wu Changshuo was known for his bold and vigorous seal inscriptions, and Huang Shiling for elegance and neatness.

Seal Character Arrangement

Seal character arrangement is achieved mainly by handling the following relationships with great finesse:

1. Thinly and densely spaced seal characters
2. Appeal and response in seal characters

Thinness and Density

This refers to the contrast between a space with densely cut lines and a space with thinly cut lines. The former constitutes the *shi* (solid) part, while the latter constitutes the *xu* (void) part. The contrast between thinness and density can increase the sense of rhythm of the inscription. Just like the use of blank space in Chinese paintings, mastery of the empty part of the seal face shows the cutter's skill.

Appeal and Response

This means coordination between or among the similar lines and structures on the seal face. It enables the characters to form an integral whole with internal relations.

Motion and Stillness

The characters on the seal face each have their dynamic or static character. The lines "in motion" are vivid, while the "still" lines are natural. The cutter has to strike a balance between motion and stillness. Excessive motion is apt to jar the viewers' perception, while too much stillness is apt to make the composition rigid.

Toughness and Gentleness

Straight lines represent toughness, and curves represent gentleness; squareness and folding represent toughness, while roundness and turning represent gentleness. Toughness should also be properly combined with gentleness in a seal inscription. Excessive toughness repels the viewer, and excessive gentleness makes for an impression of weakness.

1. Seal characters exuding both motion and stillness
2. Seal with the inscription "铜士" (*tong shi*, or Bronze Soldiers)
3. "Cohesion and dispersion" seal characters

Cohesion and Dispersion

Certain characters, lines and structures need to be placed closely together, while others need to be clearly separated. It is part of the seal cutter's art to handle these relationships properly.

Move and Make Way

This is the insertion of characters or parts of characters in the lines or structures. Moving one part of a character into the blank space of another character is called "move"; the latter then "makes way" for it. In moving or making way, make sure to keep the form of the character correct and not to make a mistake to change it to another character.

1
2
3

1. "Move and make-way" seal characters
2. "Gain and loss" seal characters
3. Edge and script in a seal

Gain and Loss

To keep the overall balance of the layout, sometimes it is necessary to change a certain part of a simplified character to its complex form. This is called "gain"; sometimes it is necessary to take off the basic structural part from a certain character or simplify part of a complex character. This is called "loss."

"Light and heavy" seal characters

Light and Heavy

A bold stroke is heavy, while a thin stroke is light. The solid part is heavy, while the blank part is light. A seal, or a character on the seal can have both lightness and heaviness.

Edge and Script

"Edge" refers to the borders of a seal, and "script" refers to the characters cut on the seal. The borders not only make the seal structure compact, they also set off the seal script.

Cutting Technique

Cutting technique is the technique of using a graver in cutting a seal. The design of the characters and the seal character arrangement is carried out through the cutting technique. On the other hand, seal cutting is done not entirely according to the design script, because cutting technique itself has its unique sense of formal beauty. The process of cutting a seal with a graver is also a process of recreation. Something called *dao qu* (cutting pleasure) is generated in this process. A good cutting technique should guide the graver as if it

Graver

“ancient simplicity.” Wen Peng of the Ming Dynasty used to get his servants to roughen the new seals he made to give them an antique look. Wu Changshuo of the Qing Dynasty used special cutting techniques to give his seals a look of ancient simplicity. But Deng Shiru kept his lines as complete, neat and clean as possible when he cut seals, and Huang Shiling in the late years of the Qing Dynasty made his seals even brighter and clearer, and created a form of clean, elegant and neat seal face. Generally speaking, lines cut with the pushing technique are neat and clean, while the lines cut with the pressing technique give an impression of ancient simplicity.

Exquisite and Free

Just like traditional Chinese painting, seal cutting also has the two styles of freehand work characterized by bold strokes and stress on spiritual resonance and the cutter’s emotions, and meticulous work characterized by close attention to detail. Of the ancient seals, the *zhu yin* (cast seal) and the *zao yin* (chiseled seal) respectively reflect the two different styles of exquisite work and freehand work. The former were neat works produced through

1 2 3

1. Seal cut by Deng Shiru, with an inscription reading, “燕翼堂” (*yan yi tang*, or Swallow Wing Hall)
2. Powerful and vigorous seal cutting style
3. Wu Changshuo’s seal cut in his later years

the processes of engraving models, making molds, and casting, while the latter were done quickly and roughly. As for the cutting techniques, the former used "double cutting," i.e. a line was cut by moving the graver back and forth, and the lines are more neat and orderly; the latter used "single cutting," i.e., a line was cut as soon as the graver was inserted, and so the lines look more spontaneous.

Beautiful and Powerful

These two styles, in fact, are the concentrated expression of all forms and elements of Chinese seals. For example, the "beautiful" style involves the double cutting technique, inscriptions cast on metal, the *xiaozhuan* characters or round relief characters, and lightness and thinness in the seal character arrangement. The powerful style involves the single cutting technique, inscriptions cut on stone, and a heavy and simple appearance.

VI

Characters on Seal Sides and Books of Seal Impressions

Biankuan (Characters on Seal Sides)

Books of Seal Impressions

Biankuan (Characters on Seal Sides)

Biankuan (characters on seal sides) refers to characters other than those cut on the seal face. Also called side characters, seal side characters, side script or *xiuzhen beike* (pocket tablet inscriptions), they form an important component part of seal art. The inscriptions can be either intaglio or relief. No seals with an inscription anywhere but on the stamping surface have been found earlier than a Sui Dynasty official seal which has chiseled on the back of it the regular intaglio characters "Made on the first day of the 10th month of the 16th year (597) of the Kaihuang reign period." Cutting characters on the sides of the stone seals was started by Wen Peng of the Ming Dynasty. He mainly used the double cutting technique. His apprentice He Zhen created the technique of single cutting, which was adopted by most seal cutters in subsequent years. In the Qing Dynasty, there were almost no seals without characters cut on the sides. The forms became more and more varied, and the contents richer and richer.

Seal-side inscription by Wen Peng: "醉倒落花前天地为衾枕" (*zui dao luo hua qian tian di wei qin zhen*, or Drunken with the falling petals, heaven and earth serve as quilt and pillow)

Seal characters on bronze ware.

The side characters mainly include the

name and age of the seal cutter, the date and place of cutting, and the owner of the seal. A bigger seal would have the source of the seal characters, the style of the face layout, source of the cutting technique, relationship with the seal owner, the process of cutting and the artistic thoughts of the artisan, and sometimes even a poem and a painting too. They were either sunken or raised, scripts or drawings, on one side or on all sides, in the corner or by the edge, cut in intaglio, in relief or in combination. They were not confined to one form or one pattern. With extremely high artistic value, such seals provide important information for later generations to determine the identity of the seal cutter and the date of cutting, and to appraise the scholarship and artistic attainments of the cutter.

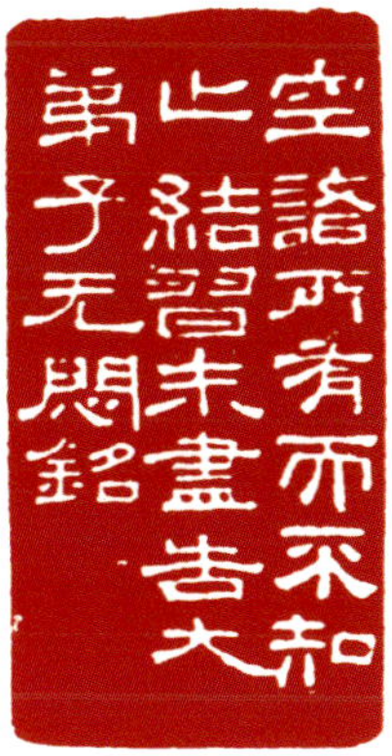

1 2
3 4

1. Seal-side characters cut in the official script.
2. Seal-side inscription by He Zhen.
3. Seal-side characters cut in the *zhuan* style.
4. Seal-side characters cut in the regular script.

Books of Seal Impressions

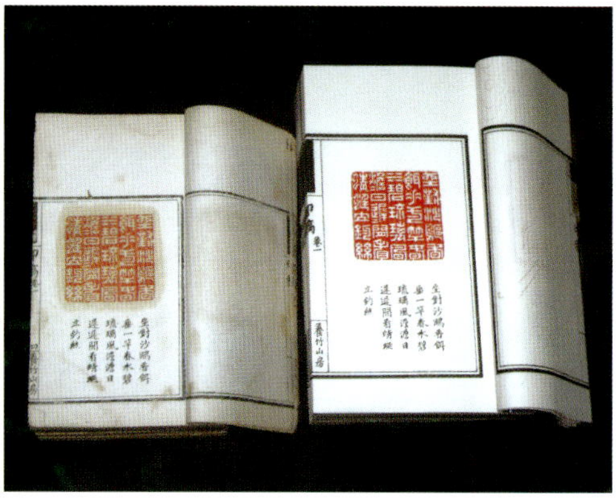

Book of seal impressions

These books provide source materials for copying or reference. They feature seals made in a certain period, of a certain school, by a certain seal cutter, in a certain region, on a certain subject or collected by a certain collector. The inscriptions collected in such books include both rubbings of the original seal inscriptions and reproductions. The former are considered more valuable.

It is generally believed that the *Xuanhe Yinpu*, or *Book of Seal Inscriptions*, of the Song Dynasty was the first book of seal inscriptions. It was compiled by Emperor Huizong (1082-1135). Unfortunately, it is no longer extant. During the Longqing reign period (1566-1572) of the Ming Dynasty, Gu Ruyou and others got together the ancient seals they had collected, and compiled the *Jigu Yinpu*, or *Collection*

Portrait of Emperor Huizong of the Song Dynasty

of Ancient Seal Inscriptions in six volumes, which contains details of more than 160 jade seals and more than 1,600 bronze seals. This collection set a precedent for collections of seal rubbings. The contents were expanded in the third year (1576) of the Wanli reign period to include 220 jade seals and 3,200 bronze seals printed on wood blocks. This book laid the foundation for similar later books in terms of compilation style, size of the sheet used and criticism of transcription of ancient texts. Apart from the *Xuanhe Yinpu*, other influential collections were *Yang's Collection of Ancient Seal Inscriptions* by Yang Yuanxiang, *Fan's Collection of Ancient Seal Inscriptions* by Fan Dache and *Seal History of Songtan Pavilion* by Guo Zongchang.

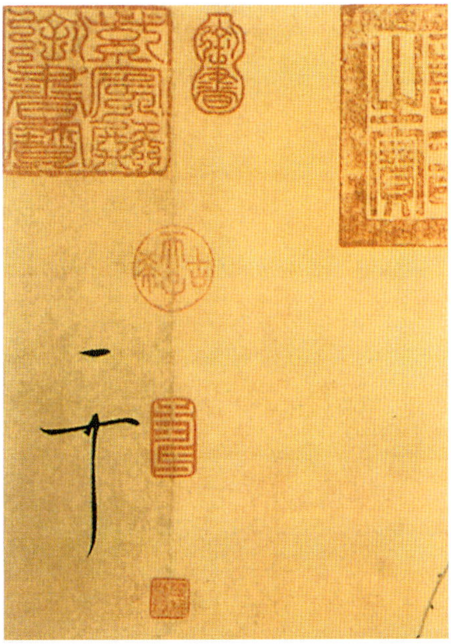

Emperor Huizong's signature

VII

Seal Cutters and Seal Society

Seal Cutters of the Ming Dynasty

Seal Cutters of the Qing Dynasty

Contemporary Seal Cutters

The Xiling Seal Society

Seal Cutters of the Ming Dynasty

Seal cutting art was greatly developed in the middle of the Ming Dynasty, and schools of different seal cutting styles emerged.

The first such school in this period was the "Sanqiao school." Its founder was Wen Peng (1498-1573, named Shoucheng and styled Sanqiao, born in Wuxian, Jiangsu Province), son of Wen Zhengming, a noted calligrapher and painter. He began to learn calligraphy and painting from his father in his childhood. At the same time, he took a keen interest in seal cutting. At that time, anther stone discovered by Wang Mian was not yet widely used, and Wen Peng often had to ask Li Wenfu, an engraver, for help in cutting his seals. One day, in his search for the ideal material for cutting seals he saw an old man hawking a "lamplight stone." This was a kind of stone used by women to make jewelry, called "*qingtian* stone." It had a fine texture and easy to engrave; Wen Peng realized

Portrait of Wen Zhengming painted by Li Yueyun of the Qing Dynasty

that this was precisely the material he needed, so he bought all the stones the old man had. He spread news of his discovery among other seal cutters, and, together with some of them, he formed the Sanqiao school, named after Wen Peng's style name. It was also called the "Wumen school" after Wen Peng's birthplace (Wuxian). This school included such important seal cutters as Gui Shichang, Li Liufang, Chen Wanyan, Gu Ling and Xu Zhonghe.

Wen Peng stands out among his peers for the attention he paid to philology in his work. As time went by, seal cutters paid less and less attention to copying the ancient characters accurately, and by the early years of the Ming Dynasty errors in seal inscriptions were commonplace. Wen Peng advocated returning to the standards of the "*Liushu*." This referred to the six sets of instructions for writing seal characters compiled in the Eastern Han Dynasty.

Wen Peng's famous seals include *Qishi'er feng shenchu* (Amid the 72 peaks) and *Qinba yisong wanhe* (Frolicking with cranes by a pine tree

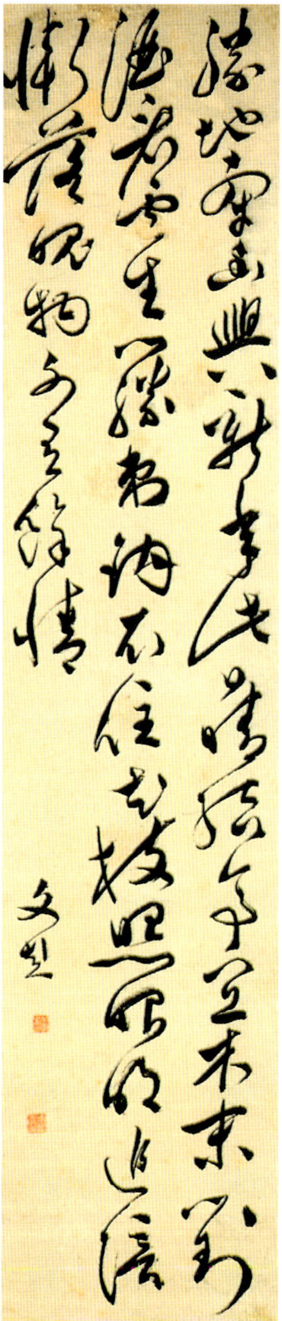

Calligraphy by Wen Peng

after playing the zither). His style is characterized by square, bold lines, after the fashion of the Han characters. It is said that after he finished cutting a seal, he would ask his servant to put it in a box and keep shaking it, so as to produce the antique effect of broken edges. Then, he would have the seals hardened by calcination for permanent keeping.

1 2

1. Seal cut by Wen Peng
2. Seal cut by He Zhen. The characters "青松白云处" (*qing song bai yun chu*) means "among green pines and white clouds."

The "Sanqiao school" was followed by the "Xueyu school," founded by He Zhen (birth date unknown, died around 1604, named Zhuchen and styled Xueyu, born in Wuyuan). He Zhen was Wen Peng's pupil and friend, and they often discussed seal cutting together. Like Wen Peng, he regarded the Han seal style as the orthodox one, and upheld the "*Liushu*" as the standard guidelines for seal cutting. At the same time, he adopted some of the fine points of the ancient characters of the Warring States Period. His seals were much more varied and he was regarded

1 2 3

1. Inscription on a seal by He Zhen: "琴罢倚松玩鹤" (*qin ba yi song wan he*) means "Frolicking with cranes by a pine tree after playing the zither."
2. Seal cut by Hu Zhengyan, an artist of the Xueyu school
3. Seal cut of the Xueyu school

1. Seal cut by He Zhen
2. Seal by Wen Peng with the inscription "文彭之印" (*wen peng zhi yin*, or Wen Peng's seal)
3. Seal cut by Su Xuan

as a "seal cutter who combines all the strengths of different styles." He also created a technique by which he cut a stroke with a single cut, leaving the cut smooth on one side but slightly rough on the other. He Zhen's fame as a seal cutter spread far and wide, and his pupils included Liang Zhi, Wu Zhong, Cheng Yuan, Cheng Pu, Jin Guangxian, Wu Jiong and Hu Zhengyan.

Wen Peng and He Zhen once worked together on a piece of *qingtian* stone for the minister of defense. The minister was so pleased with the result that he recommended them both for official positions. Later generations referred to these two masters as "Wen He." Other outstanding seal cutters of the Ming Dynasty were Su Xuan, Zhu Jian, Gan Yang and Wang Guan.

Seal Cutters of the Qing Dynasty

Achievements in research into epigraphy during the Qing Dynasty greatly benefited the art of seal cutting. The characters used on seals were no longer limited to the "*moyin* style" used on the seals cut in the Qin and Han dynasties. All characters that appeared

Cooper coin from the Tang Dynasty (618-907) with a four-character inscription on the obverse reading "kaiyuan tongbao"

Inscription on a piece of ancient bronzeware

on ancient goods and articles, including bronze wares, coins and steles, could all be used on seals. In addition, the seal cutters of the Qing Dynasty enthusiastically experimented with new cutting techniques. One of these new techniques involved the graver moving up and down slightly during the cutting process. This was judged most suitable for expressing the simplicity of the characters of remote antiquity. The seal cutters also got inspiration from calligraphic works and paintings. They "used their gravers like writing brushes," and strove for a synthesis of the arts of poetry, calligraphy, painting and seal cutting.

Cheng Sui (1605-1691), named Mu Qian and styled Soiled Taoist, was born in Shexian, Anhui Province. He became famous for his stone and bronze inscriptions, as well as calligraphy. When he first started seal cutting, the Wen He seal cutting style of the Ming Dynasty was still very popular. He carried on the tradition of stressing the Han seal style popular in the Ming Dynasty, but he put efforts into developing the esthetic values, i.e., power and poise, of seals in a creative way. This is especially manifested in his intaglio seals. His relief seals adopted pre-xiaozhuan characters

Seal cut in relief by Cheng Sui. The inscription "少壮三好音律书酒" (*shao zhuang san hao yin lü shu jiu*) means "Young and vigorous, three good things — temperament, books and wine."

from inscriptions on seals of the Warring States Period and the bronze wares of the Shang and Zhou dynasties. These inscriptions are striking for their studied unevenness. He is regarded as the founder of the "She school" among the seal cutting schools.

Lin Gao (1658-1726), named Hetian, was born in Putian, Fujian Province. He learned seal cutting under the tutorship of Wang Guan, becoming a specialist in the *moyin* style. Most of the seals of Wang Hui, a leading painter of the time, were cut by Lin Gao. However, his influence was largely confined to the two provinces of Zhejiang and Jiangsu.

The most influential seal cutter to emerge in Zhejiang Province was Ding Jing (1695-1765), also named Jingshen and born in Qiantang. His early seal cutting works were influenced by Wen Peng and He Zhen, but he made bold innovations and developed a style of his own in character writing and cutting technique. Regarding the Han seal character form which dominated the seals of the Ming Dynasty as too restrictive, he advocated wider use of ancient characters. To follow this road, he made an in-depth study of the seals made in the different dynasties. He paid special attention to the expressiveness of the cutting technique,

1 2 3

1. Seal cut by Ding Jing
2. Seal cut by Ding Jing
3. Seal cut by Qian Song, one of the "Eight Masters of Xiling." The inscription "杨季仇信印大贵大寿" (*yang ji qiu xin yin da gui da shou*) means "Yang Jiqiu's seal, great wealth and long life."

using his graver like a writing brush. He used fine, broken and short cuts in an effort to achieve the effect of flowing writing and the simplicity of metal and stone inscriptions. He assembled a number of seal cutting artists to form the "Zhejiang school." This became one of the most notable schools in the history of Chinese seals. It adopted a simplified form of the Han Dynasty's so-called clerical script to display the beauty of the structure of the seal characters more fully, including the use of broken and short cuts. The leading seal cutters of the Zhejiang school included Ding Jing, Jiang Ren, Huang Yi, Xi Gang, Chen Yuzhong, Chen Hongshou, Zhao Zhichen and Qian Song. They were also called the "Eight Masters of Xiling." Of them, the former four cutters were called the "Former Four Masters of Xiling" and the latter four cutters were called the "Latter Four Masters of Xiling." The former four followed Ding Jing, and each had his own specialty, while the latter four—except Qian Song—revealed a trend towards formulaic work.

Different from the forceful style of the Zhejiang school, the Deng school, which emerged in the middle of the Qing Dynasty, combined forcefulness with grace. Its founder was Deng Shiru (1743-1805), one of the dynasty's leading calligraphers. In his youth he spent five years studying calligraphy from tablet rubbings in the home of Mei Liu, a metal and stone inscriptions

Seal cut by Deng Shiru. The inscription "江流有声，断岸千尺" (*jiang liu you sheng, duan an qian chi*) means "The singing river flows, the banks rise up as high as one thousand feet."

collector, and copying hundreds of them, thus acquiring a good training in philology and calligraphy. He advocated "seeking seals from outside seals"; in other words, using calligraphy and literature to nourish the creative work of seal cutting. His seal cutting works have a strong flavor of calligraphy, blending the cutting technique and writing technique to create a vigorous and fluent cutting style.

1. Seal cut by Wu Rangzhi
2. Seal cut by Wu Rangzhi

More than half a century after Deng Shiru died, a successor to his cutting art carried the tradition of the Deng school forward. He was Wu Rangzhi (1799-1870, named Xizai, born in Yizheng, Jiangsu Province). When he saw Deng's works at the age of 30, he devoted himself to bringing this style to perfection. He was also a famous calligrapher, and therefore he could well understand Deng's idea of "seeking seals from outside seals." He added new content to Deng's "push cutting" technique. In the course of pushing the graver forward, he also used press cutting (a technique of cutting lines from above downward) to cut the lines, so that forceful cut marks were revealed at the turns of the strokes. Therefore, his seals had more beauty than Deng Shiru's.

Wu's seal cutting art was carried forward by Zhao Zhiqian, Wu Changshuo and Huang Shiling.

Zhao Zhiqian (1829-1884), named Huishu and styled Beian, was born in Shaoxing, Zhejiang Province. He was a creative painter and calligrapher of the late Qing Dynasty. At the same time, he also had many achievements in seal cutting to his credit. He followed Deng Shiru's creative idea of "seeking seals from outside seals." He blended the work of cutting seals with a knowledge of epigraphy and the technique of painting flowers and birds. He freely adapted the patterns of ancient characters on bronze mirrors of the Han Dynasty, the coins of the Warring States Period, the weights of the Qin Dynasty and the tablet inscriptions of the Han Dynasty to his seal cutting, greatly enriching the expressive content of Chinese seal characters. He also made many innovations in the creation of characters cut on the sides of seals.

1
2
3

1. Seal cut by Zhao Zhiqian
2. Seal cut by Zhao Zhiqian
3. Seal cut by Wu Changshuo, with an inscription reading, "且饮墨渖一升" (Just finish one liter of black ink).

Contemporary Seal Cutters

Wu Changshuo (1844-1927), also known as Jun, and Foulu, was born in Anji, Zhejiang Province. He was a master of poetry, calligraphy, painting and seal cutting. At 31 years old, he traveled widely in the adjoining provinces of Jiangsu and Zhejiang, inspecting large numbers of bronze and stone tablet rubbings, calligraphic works, paintings

Portrait of Wu Changshuo

and seal inscriptions. Later, he settled in Shanghai, where he had frequent contacts with famous calligraphers and painters, thus widening his horizons and forming a profound artistic style. He drew inspiration from inscriptions on stone blocks, sealing clay, eave tile inscriptions and inscriptions on pottery. He used the knocking, grinding and striking techniques to make his seals as simple and natural as the ancient sealing clay. He also had his own peculiar cutting technique, using his home-made graver at an obtuse angle.

The inscription on a seal cut by Qi Baishi: "今来古注闲中一意" (*jin lai gu wang xian zhong yi yi*) means "At leisure through the ages."

Huang Shiling (1849-1908), named Mufu and styled Juansou, was born in Yixian County, Anhui Province. He learned seal cutting from Wu Rangzhi, and followed

Calligraphy by Wu Changshuo

Changshuo, the *Account of the Newly-Built Guanle Pavilion of the Xiling Seal Society* contributed by Ding Ren and written by Wu Changshuo, and the *Account of Xian Spring* written by Zhang Junheng.

With a century of activities in the fields of poetry, calligraphy, painting and seal cutting, the Xiling Seal Society has become the most influential academic organization with the longest history in China. It enjoys a lofty place in the international epigraphic community. Its successive presidents have been Wu Changshuo, Ma Heng, Zhang Zongxiang, Sha Menghai, Zhao Puchu and Qi Gong.

VIII

Seal Cutting and Seal Stamping

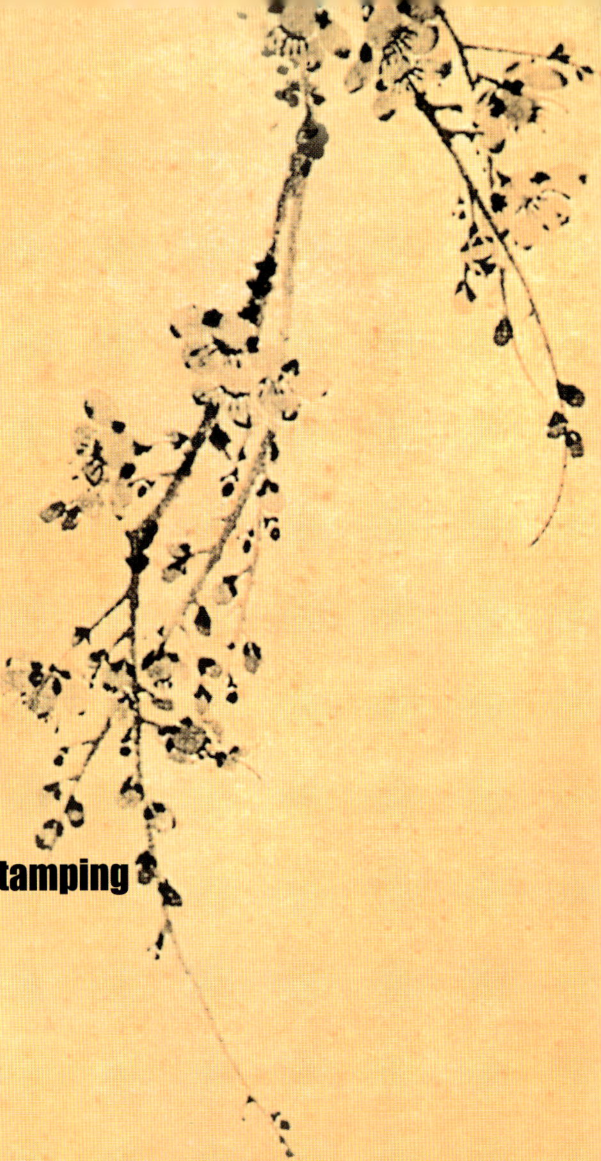

Seal Cutting

Stamping Seals

The early Chinese seals were mainly made of bronze and cast. From the Shang Dynasty to the Sui Dynasty, the characters on the seals were mainly cast together with the seal bodies. The whole process was very similar to the casting of the inscribed bronze ware, involving the carving of models, the making of molds and casting.

In the Tang Dynasty official seals were cast in bronze without inscriptions, and then the characters, in the form of bronze strips, were shaped and welded onto the seal. The lines of the characters were curved and twisting, and were therefore called *panqu xian* (twisting lines), and the seal was called *pantiao yin* (twisting bar seal).

1
2

1. Chiseled seal
2. *Pantiao* (twisting bar) seal

With the use of soft stone to make seals, the casting and welding techniques were virtually discarded. Now anyone with a few small tools could make seals, and seal making became a popular hobby.

Seal Cutting

Graver

Seal Cutting Tools

Graver: The graver used for seal cutting is usually a flat-edged blade of a certain thickness. The angle of the edge should be 40º to 20º. Two or three gravers of different sizes are needed for cutting seals of different sizes. The base of the graver should be square, so that it can be used for tapping the seal to give an antique effect of wear. To avoid the hand slipping, the graver handle should be wrapped in cotton cord. A graver with a slanting or round edge cannot be used for seal cutting.

Ink paste: The ink pastes produced in Zhangzhou, Hangzhou, Suzhou and Shanghai are considered superior. The colors of the ink pastes are cinnabar, dark brown (for an antique effect), and other suitable colors. A good ink paste must be free from seeping oil stains and have thickness and a strong covering quality. Ink paste should be kept in a porcelain box, and mixed with an ivory or plastic object from time to

Ink paste box

time.

Seal clamp: This is a tool for fixing the seal material in place while it is being worked on. Except for beginners, seal cutters usually do not use seal clamps; instead, they use the left hand to hold the seal, with the graver in the right hand, making it easier to

Brush, ink and ink slab

turn the seal flexibly.

Writing brush, ink stick and ink slab: The writing brush should be a No. 5 or No. 6 *gui* brush, and the ink should be made by rubbing an ink stick on an inkslab.

Seal gauge: This is a tool for helping to position the seal when stamping, similar to the angle rule used by a carpenter. It can be home-made. After stamping, the gauge should be kept in the same position. If the stamp is not clear, the seal should be positioned tightly against the gauge, and the stamping should be repeated.

Paper: Thin and water-absorbent *maobian* paper or *maotai* paper should be used for copying seal inscriptions, and fine paper made from bamboo or thin *xuan* paper for stamping seals. Fine paper made from bamboo should be used for taking rubbings of

Graver, seal stone and seal clamp

inscriptions.

Sandpaper and mirror: Stone for making a seal can be polished with sandpaper or on a cement floor until it is smooth (get ready iron sand, and water sand of different coarseness). A small mirror is used to reflect the seal characters the right way round, and check if they have been properly incised.

Ink mixing stick: Used for mixing ink paste, it can be an ivory or bone object, or even the plastic handle of a tooth brush. Metal articles must not be used.

Brush: An old toothbrush or an old painting brush can be used to clean stone dust from the face of the seal before stamping.

Steps for Cutting Seals

The seal cutting process begins with the layout of the seal face, including the inscription. Then the material for the seal is chosen. This is cut and trimmed, and finally the name of the cutter is added.

Seal script written on absorbent paper

Sometimes, the layout process has to be repeated up to 200 times before it is regarded as satisfactory.

After the layout is decided, there are usually two ways of writing characters on the seal face.

On the basis of the prepared inscription, the characters are written inversely on the seal face. Only veteran seal cutters can write inverted characters well. A beginner may write the inscription on very thin paper, so that the ink marks are permeable on the back of the paper, showing the characters in inverted form. The marks on the back of the paper are then copied onto the seal.

Push cutting

The other way is to press the seal on the paper to form a square within which to write the inscription. Then wet the seal face lightly with water, and press the paper with the inscription face-downward onto the seal face. In this position, the paper should be rubbed hard with a fingernail or hard tool. The ink marks, with the characters in reverse, should then adhere to the seal face when the paper is removed. To make the script more distinct, make sure to prepare new and thick ink and polish the seal face with a piece of sandpaper, making it easier for the ink to stick on it.

The third step is to cut and trim the lines. Choose a suitable cutting technique as required for the script. For example, to cut a joint between two strokes, it's better to use the press cutting technique. To cut a powerful long stroke, it's preferable to use the

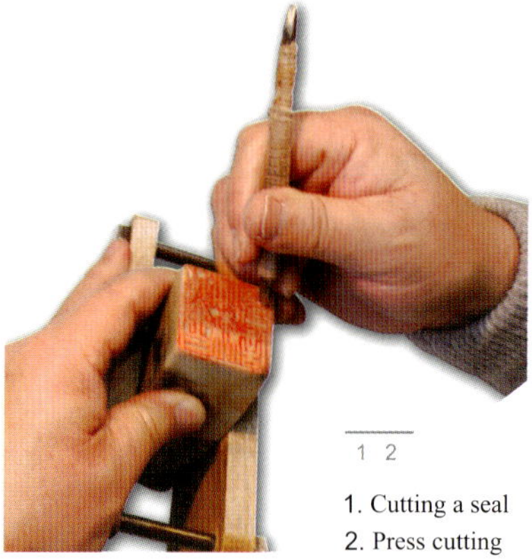

1. Cutting a seal
2. Press cutting

push cutting technique.

After a seal is cut, "filling powder" is used to check if it has been cut well. This powder is produced when the seal is polished—usually white. It is kept carefully in a small box for the purpose of filling the sunken background of the inscription immediately after a seal has been cut. In this way, any part of the inscription which is not distinct, and any part of the background that has not been cut away properly, can be seen clearly, and remedied. A small mirror can be placed below the seal to reflect the inscription as it will appear on a stamped document, to find out whether there is anything that needs to be improved.

The fourth step is to handle the borders of the seal face layout. In this respect, seals generally fall into two categories. One consists of works done with meticulous care and fine, delicate strokes; the other is freehand-cut works. The former must have both the characters and the borders cut with meticulous care and fine strokes. If the characters are colorful and mottled, the borders should naturally match them. Traditionally, seals have followed the principle of harmony. Before the Qin Dynasty and the unification of China, seal characters were natural, and the borders of the seals were plain and simple. In the Qin and Han dynasties, seals gradually became neat and orderly, with correspondingly neat and orderly borders. The borders of seals with characters cut in relief are externally round and internally square, while the borders of seals with characters cut in intaglio are rounded off by removing the corners.

The fifth step is to remove the background. The space on the seal face other than the characters are red after stamping if the characters are cut in intaglio, and white if the characters are cut in relief. The white spaces are dug out after the seal characters are cut. The cutting away of the background between the characters is called "excavating the ground." Generally speaking, there are three ways of doing this:

Flat ground: If the ground is to be made flat and smooth, as in ivory and horn materials, deep-cutting gravers are used.

Sesame ground: When blotches like sesame seeds are to be made to appear in the spaces between the characters, the press cutting technique is used throughout.

Wavy ground: The push cutting technique leaves marks like waves.

After the inscription is cut, the name of the cutter is placed on the left side.

Ink paste applied gently to a seal face

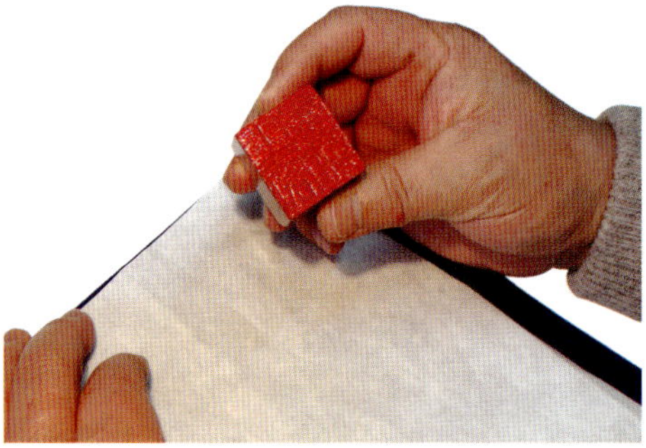

Cinnabar should be applied evenly to the whole seal face.

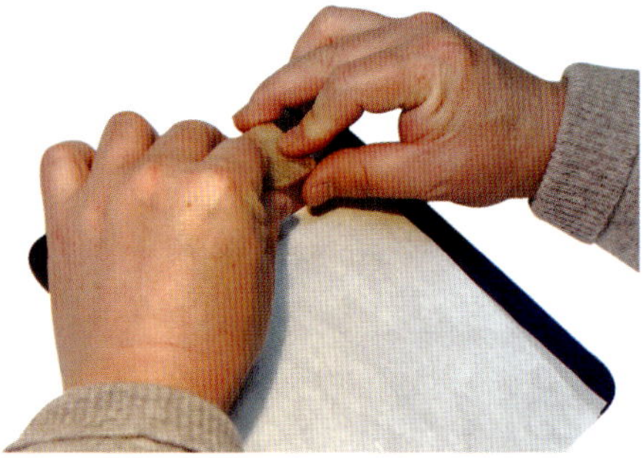

Seal stamping

Stamping Seals

After a seal is cut, the seal stone is cleaned of ink stains and stone dust with a tooth brush and detergent.

After cleaning the seal face and before stamping, get the paper, ink paste and seal clamp ready. The paper chosen should be fine, even and flat, and its surface smooth. Dip the seal face evenly in the ink paste. Hold the ink paste box in the left hand, and press the seal face onto the ink paste lightly. The cinnabar contained in the ink paste is attached to the seal face by the oil in the ink. However, if the cinnabar is not fine enough, or if the ink oil is not thick and sticky enough or is too thin or too dry, the cinnabar will not stick evenly to the seal face. In such a case, the ink paste has to be prepared again.

The seal face must be dipped in the ink paste evenly so that the whole seal face is covered with cinnabar. Then pause when the seal is about to touch the paper at the place where the seal is to be affixed. Correct the bearing of the seal to ensure that it is level and upright, and then stamp the seal down quickly when it is about one centimeter from the paper. Press it with force, but do not shake or move it. If a seal is used too long, the face may no longer be smooth, and the edges may become worn. In this case, after the seal is on the paper, keep it on the original position and press it on the four edges with a slight tilt to get the proper effect.

Seals are stamped sometimes as required by the nature of the seal characters. If the seal characters are cut by freehand cutters, such as seals by Wu Changshuo and Qi Baishi, thick ink paste and heavy stamping are required. Light force and thin ink paste are good enough for the delicate seal faces. If the latter seals are stamped heavily with thick ink paste, the stamped seal characters will not be as distinct as desired. Moreover, light force should be applied for seal characters cut in relief, and heavier force for characters cut on seals in intaglio.

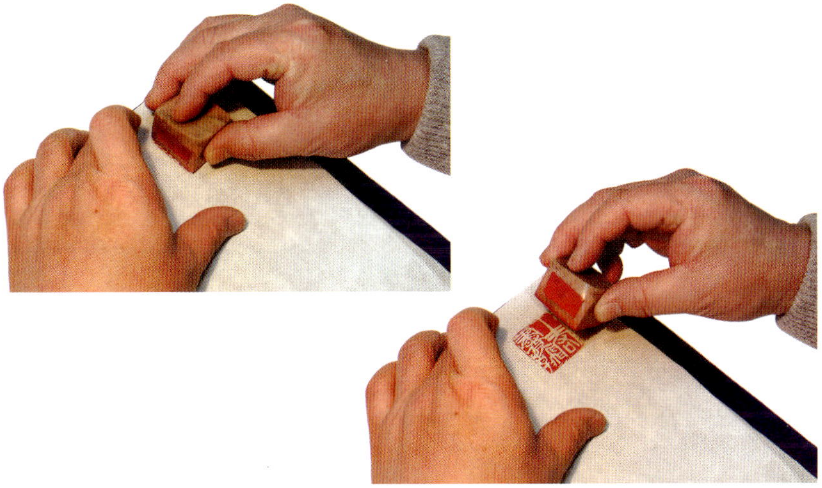

1
2

1. Seal stamping
2. Correctly stamped seal with clear characters

After it is used, a seal should be cleaned with cotton and kept for use again. Seal collectors often make embroidered boxes for keeping seals, but frequently-used seals cannot be taken out of the boxes and cleaned every time they are used; therefore some people find it unnecessary to clean seals frequently, thinking that the old ink left on the seal increases the sense of simplicity and unaffectedness.

Appendix:

Chronological Table of the Chinese Dynasties

Dynasty		Period
Xia		About the end of the 22nd century BC to the early 17th century BC
Shang		About the 17th century BC to the 11th century BC
Western Zhou		About the 11th century BC to 771 BC
Eastern Zhou	Spring and Autumn Period	770BC-476BC
	Warring States Period	475BC-221BC
Qin		221 BC-206 BC
Han	Western Han Eastern Han	206 BC-25 AD 25-220
Three Kingdoms	Wei	220-265
	Shu Han	221-263
	Wu	222-280
Jin	Western Jin Eastern Jin	265-317 317-420
Sixteen Kingdoms		304-439
Southern and Northern Dynasties		420-589
Sui		581-618
Tang		618-907
Five Dynasties and Ten States		907-960
Song	Northern Song Southern Song	960-1127 1127-1279
Yuan		1206-1368
Ming		1368-1644
Qing		1616-1911

图书在版编目（CIP）数据

中国印/牛克诚编著.
—北京：外文出版社, 2005
ISBN 978-7-119-04197-1
I. 中… II.牛… III.印章－基本知识
－中国－英文 IV.J292.4
中国版本图书馆CIP数据核字（2005）第096144号

英文翻译：章挺权
英文审定：Paul White　贺　军
责任编辑：刘芳念
装帧设计：华审书装
印刷监制：韩少乙

中国印

作　　者：牛克诚
图片提供：王士宏　等

出版发行：
外文出版社出版（中国北京百万庄大街24号）
邮政编码：100037
网　　址：www.flp.com.cn
电　　话：008610-68320579（总编室）
008610-68995852（发行部）
008610-68327750（版权部）
印　　刷：
北京外文印刷厂
开本：787mm × 1092mm　1/16　　印张：6
2009年第1版第2次印刷
(英)
ISBN 978-7-119-04197-1
07800(平)
85-E-591 P